THE FINESSE

ONLY A LAST RESORT

Jᴀᴍᴇs Mᴀʀsʜ Sᴛᴇʀɴʙᴇʀɢ MD (Dʀ. J)

authorHOUSE

AuthorHouse™
1663 Liberty Drive
Bloomington, IN 47403
www.authorhouse.com
Phone: 833-262-8899

Published by AuthorHouse 04/16/2021

ISBN: 978-1-6655-1583-2 (sc)
ISBN: 978-1-6655-1582-5 (e)

Library of Congress Control Number: 2021902084

THIS BOOK IS DEDICATED TO

THE MEMORY OF

MY PARENTS

EMIL AND LEONORE
STERNBERG

CONTENTS

ACKNOWLEDGEMENTS

This book would not have been possible without the help of several friends. Frank Stewart, Michael Lawrence, Anne Lund, Eddie Kantar, and Marty Bergen all provided suggestions for material for the book.

I am forever indebted to Hall of Famer Fred Hamilton and the late Bernie Chazen, without whose guidance and teaching I would not have achieved whatever success I have had in bridge.

I want to thank my editor Randy Baron for his valuable assistance. Any errors in the books are totally mine.

And of course I want to thank Vickie Lee Bader, whose love and patience helped guide me thru the many hours of this endeavor.

James Marsh Sternberg MD
Palm Beach Gardens FL

INTRODUCTION

How much do you really know about finesses, one of the most common techniques in bridge and yet one of the most abused. The term "finesseaholic" describes a player who never met a finesse he/she didn't want to take. So often the finesse is really a LAST RESORT, only when other more promising lines of play are not available or have failed.

As a common technique, so much is often taken for granted. Often there are questions that need be resolved. Is it a two-way guess? Which suit should be finessed first? Which hand is it safe to finesse into? Which card should be led may make the difference between success and failure. Are there clues in the bidding or lack of bidding?

One definition of "experience" is what we get when we don't get what we want. After you play bridge for a while, you will learn that the finesses you desperately need to work are the ones that fail. Profit from experience. Avoid an unnecessary finesse that may lead to disaster if it loses.

Bridge is a hand, not an isolated suit. Just because a finesse is possible does not mean you have to take it. While it may be the right way to play that particular suit, it may not be the right way to play the bridge hand.

This book is divided into chapters, but there is a lot of overlap. Choosing which suit to finesse to set up a second suit could belong in "Which Finesse?" or "Second Suit." And "Timing", a chapter itself, plays a role in most chapters. The hands are not really a quiz; you can see all four hands, but cover the East/West hands and see how you do.

Big Clue: It's always good to be the "other declarer".

A QUICK FINESSE QUIZ PART I

What is the best way to play the following combinations? Assume declarer has plenty of entries.

1. A J 9 4	2. Q 10 6 4	3. A K J 5 3	4. A K 10 9
6 3 2	K 5 3	10 7 6 2	8 3

5. K 8 3 2	6. 6 4 2
Q 10 7 6 4	K 10 9 8

1. Lead low and finesse the nine. If this loses to the King or Queen, finesse the Jack on the second round. This is better than finessing the Jack on the first round since West is more likely to have K 10 or Q 10 than K Q.

2. Lead low to the King, intending to finesse the 10 next. This is the general principle of leading towards the unsupported high card first, reserving the 10 for the second round. This saves a trick when an opponent may have a singleton honor.

3. Cask the A-K, the percentage play with nine cards in the suit.

4. Lead low to the 9, then low to the 10. South has an approximately 75% chance of taking three tricks.

5. Lead low to the King. If West follows and East wins the Ace, play the Queen next with nine cards.

6. Lead low from dummy and finesse the 10. If this loses to the Queen or Jack, lead low from dummy again and finesse again. It is more likely East began with the Queen or Jack than West began with both honors.

A FINESSE QUIZ PART II

Now you are finessing against West. How should you proceed?

7. A 10 4 2	8. A Q 9 5 4	9. A 10 9 2	10. A K 10 8
Q J 5 3	J 7 6 3 2	J 4 3	J 5 4 3

7. Lead low and finesse the ten. South cannot afford to lead high on the first round if West has the singleton King. If the 10 wins, South enters his hand and leads an honor.

8. Lead the Jack. With ten cards, the high lead cannot cost. To lead low to the queen will leave West a trick if he started with K 10 x.

9. Lead low and finesse the nine. If it loses, lead low again and finesse the ten. Do not lead the Jack which will cost a trick if West started with s singleton or doubleton honor.

10. Cash the Ace, then enter the South hand and lead the Jack. South can afford here to guard against East having the singleton Queen. If East follows low, South must lead the Jack on the second round.

If he leads low and finesses the 10, West will make a trick with Q 9 x x.

TIMING

TIMING: NO FINESSE

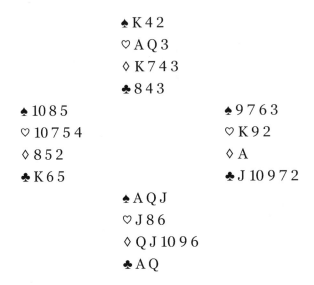

♠K 4 2
♥A Q 3
♦K 7 4 3
♣8 4 3

♠10 8 5   ♠9 7 6 3
♥10 7 5 4   ♥K 9 2
♦8 5 2   ♦A
♣K 6 5   ♣J 10 9 7 2

♠A Q J
♥J 8 6
♦Q J 10 9 6
♣A Q

Contract: 3 NT
Opening Lead: ♥4

Declarer had visions of lots of tricks. If everything went well, twelve tricks were possible. And being of the mindset of "I never met a finesse I didn't like," played low at trick one.

East won the king and shifted to a club. Twelve quickly became eight.

Question: What should have declarer been thinking about?

At the other table, the opening lead was the same. This declarer grabbed the heart ace and started racing for home. After giving up a diamond, he was playing for overtricks, if there were any.

It's good to think about what could go wrong before, not after it happens.

TIMING: NO FINESSES

```
                        ♠ 10 6 4
                        ♡ Q 6 2
                        ◊ A 10 3
                        ♣ J 4 3 2
        ♠ 2                             ♠ J 8 7
        ♡ K J 10 9 4                    ♡ A 8 7
        ◊ Q 6 5 2                       ◊ J 9 7
        ♣ A Q 9                         ♣ 8 7 6 5
                        ♠ A K Q 9 5 3
                        ♡ 5 3
                        ◊ K 8 4
                        ♣ K 10
```

South	West	North	East
1 ♠	2 ♡	2 ♠	3 ♡
3 ♠		All Pass	

Opening Lead: ♡ Jack

The heart jack won the first trick. West continued a heart to East's ace, declarer ruffed the third heart. After drawing trumps, declarer was looking at two potential losers in clubs and one in diamonds.

He played a diamond to the dummy and led a low club to his ten. This must have been a 'practice' finesse because even if he set up a club trick, he had no dummy entry to use it. All those potential losers became real ones. Down one.

Question: Could you have timed this better (after being given an opportunity)?

After drawing trumps, declarer is 'a step ahead' by just leading the club king from his hand. He can win the diamond return in hand and lead the club ten.

The jack of clubs is good for a diamond discard, and the ace of diamonds is still there as an entry.

Given an opportunity? Yes, East knew the third heart was not cashing and should have started attacking the diamonds. At that time, it was the defense that was 'a step ahead'.

FINESSE? TIMING

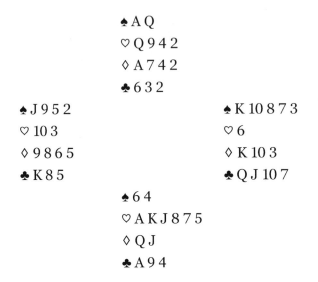

```
                    ♠ A Q
                    ♡ Q 9 4 2
                    ◊ A 7 4 2
                    ♣ 6 3 2
     ♠ J 9 5 2                        ♠ K 10 8 7 3
     ♡ 10 3                           ♡ 6
     ◊ 9 8 6 5                        ◊ K 10 3
     ♣ K 8 5                          ♣ Q J 10 7
                    ♠ 6 4
                    ♡ A K J 8 7 5
                    ◊ Q J
                    ♣ A 9 4
```

Contract: 4 ♡

Opening Lead: ♠ 2

Declarer, concerned he might have four losers, took a spade finesse at trick one. He felt he had a 75% chance since he needed one out of two finesses to be successful. East won and shifted to a club. When the diamond finesse lost, (you knew that was coming), the defense cashed two clubs. Down one.

"Partner, you started with ten tricks, what happened?", asked North.

Question: What was North referring to? The other declarer made four hearts.

The other declarer counted six trumps, one spade, one club, and two diamonds. But as so often happens, it was going to be a race to the finish line. And right now, who was ahead? The good guys, North/South.

This declarer won the spade ace, drew trumps, and took a diamond finesse. It lost but now declarer had ten tricks when that club came flying his way from East. Six hearts, one spade, one club, and two diamonds.

FINESSE? TIMING

```
                        ♠ 10 8
                        ♡ A 8 5
                        ◊ A 8 7
                        ♣ A J 5 4 2
         ♠ 6 4 3                        ♠ K Q J 9 7 5
         ♡ J 10 7 6                     ♡ ----
         ◊ Q 6 5 3                      ◊ K J 10 9
         ♣ 9 7                          ♣ Q 10 8
                        ♠ A 2
                        ♡ K Q 9 4 3 2
                        ◊ 4 2
                        ♣ K 6 3
```

North	East	South	West
1 ♣	1 ♠	2 ♡	P
3 ♡	P	4 ♡	All Pass

Opening Lead: ♠ 3

Declarer won the ace and cashed the three high trumps. He played the club king, then led a club to the jack. East won, cashed a spade, and shifted to the jack of diamonds.

Declarer won and led the club ace. West ruffed and cashed a diamond.

Down one.

Question: Could you have timed this better to make four hearts?

The other declarer tried to stay a step ahead. He won the opening spade lead and cashed three high trumps. But then he cashed the A-K of clubs, feeling the finesse was likely to lose and give the timing back to the defense.

Then he conceded a club. East cashed a spade and shifted to diamonds. Declarer won the ace and discarded his last diamond on the good club.

He lost one spade, one heart, and one club.

NO FINESSES, TAKE YOUR NINE AND GO HOME

```
                    ♠ Q J 9 8 3
                    ♡ J 5
                    ◊ A J 3
                    ♣ Q 10 6
      ♠ 5 2                          ♠ A 7 6 4
      ♡ A K 10 2                     ♡ 6 4 3
      ◊ 7 6 5 2                      ◊ K 9 8
      ♣ 8 7 3                        ♣ 9 4 2
                    ♠ K 10
                    ♡ Q 9 8 7
                    ◊ Q 10 4
                    ♣ A K J 5
```

Contract: 3 NT
Opening Lead: ◊ 7

The first declarer instinctively took a finesse at trick one, not picturing what might go wrong. East showed him, winning the diamond king and switching to a heart. Now the timing was in favor of the defenders, no longer the declarer.

West won the heart king and returned the deuce. The jack in dummy won, but when declarer started the spades, East won and continued hearts.
Down one.

Question: How did declarer let this one get away? So many potential tricks.

The other declarer, with the same opening lead, played the ace. No finesse, thank you. He forced out the spade ace and had nine tricks. Four spades, four clubs, and one diamond. What's the problem?

FINESSE? NO, BLOCK THEIR SUIT

```
                    ♠ J 8 5 4 3
                    ♡ A Q
                    ◊ Q 9 2
                    ♣ J 6 4
    ♠ Q 5 2                            ♠ 10 9 6
    ♡ X X 7 6 4                        ♡ X 8
    ◊ K 6                              ◊ 7 5 3
    ♣ 10 9 2                           ♣ Q 8 7 5 3
                    ♠ A K
                    ♡ 9 5 3 2
                    ◊ A J 10 8 4
                    ♣ A K
```

Contract: 3 NT
Opening Lead: ♡ 6

Declarer # 1 finessed the queen at trick one. He later lost a diamond finesse.

Question: How did the above declarer do? What did you play at trick one?

The other declarer, # 2, won the ace at trick one and lost a diamond finesse.

Let's look at four possibilities: Think about the opening lead. East rates to have an honor card. Two scenarios:

Declarer # 1. East had the heart king and returned a heart. Down one.
Declarer # 1. West had the heart king. The declarer made 3 NT
Declarer # 1 made 3 NT half the time, depending on who had the heart king.

Declarer # 2. East had the heart king, but the suit was blocked. He made 3 NT.
Declarer # 2. West had the heart king. West could only cash two more tricks, the
                nine was a big card. He made 3 NT.
The other declarer, # 2, made 3 NT both times by not finessing, regardless of who had the heart king.

How did you do?

TIMING: TO FINESSE OR NOT TO FINESSE

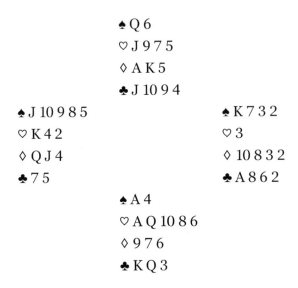

Contract: 4 ♡

Opening Lead: ♠ Jack

The first trick went queen, king, ace. Declarer crossed to the ace of diamonds to take a trump finesse. West won the king, cashed the spade ten and returned the diamond queen.

When East won the club ace, she returned a diamond to West for the setting trick. Down one.

Question: What was a better plan to make four hearts?

At the other table, declarer realized the heart finesse was an illusion. There were ten tricks even if the trump finesse was wrong. One spade, four hearts, two diamonds, and three clubs provided South kept his dummy entries.

Just draw trumps, by starting with the ace. This gave declarer the tempo and entries to set up the clubs and take ten tricks.

NO FINESSE, TAKE YOUR TRICKS

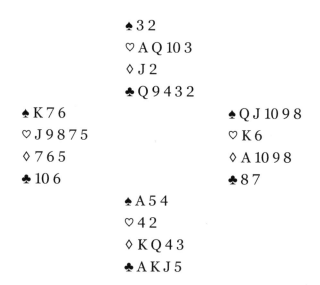

```
                    ♠ 3 2
                    ♡ A Q 10 3
                    ◊ J 2
                    ♣ Q 9 4 3 2
    ♠ K 7 6                        ♠ Q J 10 9 8
    ♡ J 9 8 7 5                    ♡ K 6
    ◊ 7 6 5                        ◊ A 10 9 8
    ♣ 10 6                         ♣ 8 7
                    ♠ A 5 4
                    ♡ 4 2
                    ◊ K Q 4 3
                    ♣ A K J 5
```

Contract: 3 NT
Opening Lead: ♡ 7

Declarer, in a Swiss team game, could count nine winners: five clubs, one heart, one spade, and two diamonds after driving out the diamond ace. But she couldn't resist playing that heart queen. You could almost hear North's teeth gnashing.

Of course, West had the heart king and switched to spades. Whatever happened to those nine tricks we will never know. Down two.

Question: Would you have taken your nine tricks and gotten out of Dodge?

You bet. The declarer at the other table grabbed the heart ace and drove out the diamond ace. At least nine tricks, thank you.

Perhaps playing in a pair game with matchpoint scoring, South could have an excuse for risking the heart finesse.

STAYING ONE STEP AHEAD, NO EARLY FINESSE

```
                    ♠ K J 5
                    ♡ A K 8
                    ♢ J 5 3
                    ♣ A Q J 9
    ♠ 9 7 4 3                      ♠ Q 10 2
    ♡ 6 4                          ♡ Q 9 7 5 2
    ♢ 8 6 4 2                      ♢ A 9 7
    ♣ 6 5 2                        ♣ K 7
                    ♠ A 8 6
                    ♡ J 10 3
                    ♢ K Q 10
                    ♣ 10 8 4 3
```

Contract: 3 NT
Opening Lead: ♡ 6

West led a heart, hoping to find his partner's suit. Declarer, seeing at least three clubs, and two in every other suit, quickly played low without much concern. East won and returned a heart.

Declarer came to his hand with the spade ace and took a club finesse. East won and played another heart. Play slowed considerably, as declarer's concern rose. Declarer led a diamond. Nine had been compressed into eight.

Question: What was the major cause of this?

Poor timing. The other declarer won the heart ace at trick one. After the losing club finesse, East had no winning options. A spade or heart return would cost a trick.

If East safely returned a club, declarer could just drive out the diamond ace and have at least nine tricks.

TIMING: NO TIME FOR FINESSES

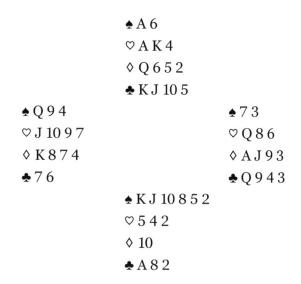

♠ A 6
♡ A K 4
◊ Q 6 5 2
♣ K J 10 5

♠ Q 9 4
♡ J 10 9 7
◊ K 8 7 4
♣ 7 6

♠ 7 3
♡ Q 8 6
◊ A J 9 3
♣ Q 9 4 3

♠ K J 10 8 5 2
♡ 5 4 2
◊ 10
♣ A 8 2

Contract: 4 ♠
Opening Lead: ♡ Jack

Declarer won the opening lead. He cashed the ace of trumps and led a trump to the jack. West won and returned another heart. Declarer won, drew the last trump, and led a club to the jack.

East won and cashed the diamond ace and the heart queen. Down one.

Question: The Society of Finessers were proud of declarer. Are you?

Frank Stewart would have said, "Gentlemen, let me give you something to complain about." No finesses.

The other declarer saw an issue of timing. He had one fast loser, a diamond, but two slow losers, a heart and a club. To stay ahead of the defense, he won the opening lead and cashed the A-K of trumps. Then he cashed the A-K of clubs and led the club jack.

The defense won, but declarer now had the timing to discard his heart loser on the club ten. He lost one spade, one diamond, and one club.

TIMING: NO FINESSES

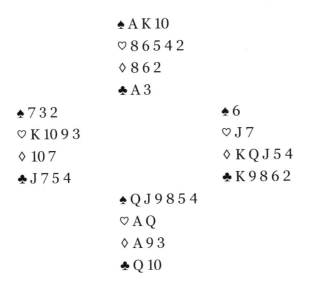

```
                    ♠ A K 10
                    ♡ 8 6 5 4 2
                    ◊ 8 6 2
                    ♣ A 3
        ♠ 7 3 2                      ♠ 6
        ♡ K 10 9 3                   ♡ J 7
        ◊ 10 7                       ◊ K Q J 5 4
        ♣ J 7 5 4                    ♣ K 9 8 6 2
                    ♠ Q J 9 8 5 4
                    ♡ A Q
                    ◊ A 9 3
                    ♣ Q 10
```

Contract: 4 ♠

Opening Lead: ♣ 4

With four possible losers, declarer played low at trick one taking the club finesse. East won and returned a diamond. The four possible losers became real losers.

Down one. North asked, "Is there ever a finesse you don't take?"

Question: What was North referring to? Could you have timed this better?

The other declarer was not about to let the defense get ahead. The club queen was a 'mirage'. There were more important matters. He won the opening lead and started the hearts, ace, then queen, giving up another finesse, a "queen mirage." This was the same way he would have played if both queens had been deuces.

The defense won, cashed a club and switched to diamonds, but it was too late. Declarer was in control. He went to dummy with a trump. When both opponents followed, the hand was cold. He ruffed a heart, went back to dummy with another trump, and ruffed another heart.

The last spade in dummy was the entry to the established good heart. Declarer discarded one of his diamond losers on the heart. Ten tricks.

FINESSE OR NO FINESSE? TIMING

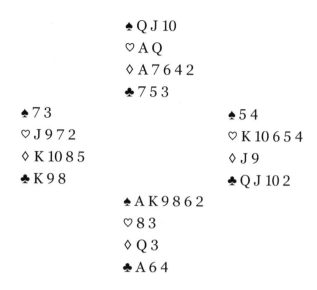

♠ Q J 10
♥ A Q
♦ A 7 6 4 2
♣ 7 5 3

♠ 7 3
♥ J 9 7 2
♦ K 10 8 5
♣ K 9 8

♠ 5 4
♥ K 10 6 5 4
♦ J 9
♣ Q J 10 2

♠ A K 9 8 6 2
♥ 8 3
♦ Q 3
♣ A 6 4

Contract: 4 ♠
Opening Lead: ♥ 2

So much in bridge is timing. Declarer took a heart finesse at trick one. East won and shifted to the club queen. Declarer ducked and won the club continuation, as West unblocked his king.

After drawing trumps, declarer had nowhere to go. He lost another club and a diamond, down one.

Question: What plan would you have tried instead?

Hand pattern recognition is so important. You can't reach your destination if you don't have some idea of the way there. What kind of hand is this?

A second suit, but you have to be a step ahead. So to keep on track, you should grab that first trick and start the second suit before, not after, the club ace is dislodged.

Win the heart ace and play ace and a diamond, the way you would if the diamond queen, another 'mirage', were a deuce. Now you are out in front, and using the trumps as entries, can set up that last diamond in time to discard a club loser.

TIMING: WHO GOES FIRST

```
                    ♠ A K 6
                    ♡ 9 4 3 2
                    ◇ 4 3 2
                    ♣ A Q 9
      ♠ Q J 10 8 4                      ♠ 9 5 3
      ♡ K                               ♡ J 10 8
      ◇ 10 8 6 5                        ◇ K J 9 7
      ♣ 8 6 3                           ♣ 7 5 2
                    ♠ 7 2
                    ♡ A Q 7 6 5
                    ◇ A Q
                    ♣ K J 10 4
```

Contract: 6 ♡

Opening Lead: ♠ Queen

Where to begin? The first declarer won the opening lead in dummy and led a small heart. East played low. She played the queen.

Question: Was this the right play? If not, what was?

The other declarer asked himself how many heart tricks he needed, four or five? He didn't know, because he didn't know if he had a diamond loser. There is more than one way to play A Q x x x opposite x x x x.

He took the diamond finesse first. It won. Now what? Or it lost. Now what?

If it won, you needed four heart tricks. How should you play the hearts? Cash the ace, then lead to the queen. A safety play for a singleton king with West.

If it lost, you needed five heart tricks. How should you play the hearts? Lead towards the queen first, hoping for Kx in East.

FINESSE OR NOT? SAME EITHER WAY BUT TIMING

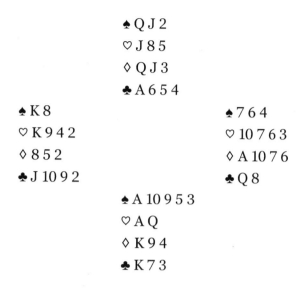

```
              ♠ Q J 2
              ♡ J 8 5
              ◊ Q J 3
              ♣ A 6 5 4
♠ K 8                        ♠ 7 6 4
♡ K 9 4 2                    ♡ 10 7 6 3
◊ 8 5 2                      ◊ A 10 7 6
♣ J 10 9 2                   ♣ Q 8
              ♠ A 10 9 5 3
              ♡ A Q
              ◊ K 9 4
              ♣ K 7 3
```

Contract: 4 ♠

Opening Lead: ♣ Jack

Declarer won the opening lead with the ace and took a heart finesse. West won and continued clubs. Declarer lost a trick in each suit. Down one.

Question: Could declarer have prevented this? How would you have played?

The other declarer saw the need to try to get rid of his slow club loser. Entries to the dummy were scarce. He won the opening lead in hand. The heart finesse was another mirage.

He played the heart ace, then the queen. He now had both the timing and the entry to the heart jack to discard the club loser. Anything else was a bonus.

Notice how many heart tricks the second declarer took? Two. Had he taken a finesse in hearts, he would have taken two heart tricks, no matter who had the king. But the timing, ah, there's the difference.

WHICH FINESSE? OTHER WORK FIRST

```
                    ♠ J 9 8
                    ♡ Q J 2
                    ◊ Q J 3
                    ♣ A 8 5 4
        ♠ K 5 4 2                    ♠ 10 7 6 3
        ♡ K 8                        ♡ 6 5 4
        ◊ 8 5 2                      ◊ A 10 6 4
        ♣ J 10 9 2                   ♣ Q 6
                    ♠ A Q
                    ♡ A 10 9 7 3
                    ◊ K 9 7
                    ♣ K 7 3
```

Contract: 4 ♡

Opening Lead: ♣ Jack

Declarer won the opening lead in dummy and took a trump finesse. West won and continued clubs. Declarer drew trumps and took a spade finesse.

"Too bad there are not any more finesses for you to take," thought North as he wrote -100, losing a trick in each suit.

Question: What do you think the North player was writing at the other table?

The other declarer, seeing a possible loser in each suit, was more concerned about avoiding one of the losers. She won the opening club lead in hand and played ace and then the queen (another 'mirage') of spades.

West won, but now declarer had the spade jack as a parking place for her club loser. +620, losing only one spade, one heart, and one diamond.

NO FINESSE, LISTEN TO THE BIDDING

```
              ♠ A 10 6 5 4
              ♡ Q 7 6
              ◊ A Q 7
              ♣ 9 2
    ♠ Q 3                      ♠ K J 9
    ♡ 4 2                      ♡ 9 5 3
    ◊ J 10 9 8 5 4             ◊ K 3
    ♣ A 10 4                   ♣ 8 7 6 5 3
              ♠ 8 7 2
              ♡ A K J 10 8
              ◊ 6 2
              ♣ K Q J
```

West	North	East	South
2 ◊	P	P	2 ♡
P	4 ♡	All Pass	

Opening Lead: ◊ Jack

Declarer was facing four possible losers: Two spades, one diamond, and one club. She took a diamond finesse at trick one. East won the king and returned the suit. The four losers came true. Down one.

Question: How did declarer at the other table make four spades?

The diamond finesse can wait. There is more important work to be done. Win the diamond ace and draw trumps. Now lead a diamond.

If West plays the king, the queen is good to discard a spade loser. If West plays low, duck. East is most likely down to a singleton king and again the queen is good for a discard.

FINESSE AT TRICK ONE? SUFFER THE CONSEQUENCES

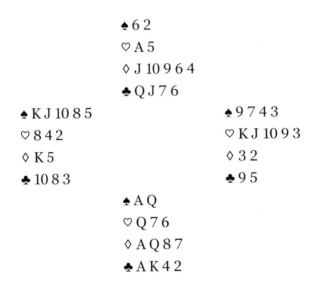

```
                        ♠ 6 2
                        ♡ A 5
                        ◊ J 10 9 6 4
                        ♣ Q J 7 6
        ♠ K J 10 8 5                    ♠ 9 7 4 3
        ♡ 8 4 2                         ♡ K J 10 9 3
        ◊ K 5                           ◊ 3 2
        ♣ 10 8 3                        ♣ 9 5
                        ♠ A Q
                        ♡ Q 7 6
                        ◊ A Q 8 7
                        ♣ A K 4 2
```

Contract: 3 NT
Opening Lead: ♡ 8

The first declarer looking at the opening lead, pictured a possible holding like ♡ K J 9 8 in West's hand and played low. Whether this was good or bad technique remains a moot question. The roof caved in.

East won the king (finesse # 1) and returned a spade. Declarer played the queen, West won the king (finesse # 2) and continued spades. Declarer went to dummy and took a diamond finesse, losing to West's king (finesse # 3). Down two.

Question: Since ten tricks were there, which finesses would you avoid?

The declarer in the other room took the ace at trick one. No finesse, thank you. She started on diamonds, losing to the king. But East was the danger hand; West could not attack declarer's guarded ♡ Q 7.

Another heart return meant eleven tricks for declarer, better than the seven in the first room.

TIMING: THE FINESSE CAN WAIT

                          ♠ K J 6
                          ♡ Q 10 9 4
                          ◊ K 6
                          ♣ Q 10 9 5
        ♠ 10 9 8 5 2   ♠ Q 3
        ♡ A 8 6   ♡ 7 5 2
        ◊ Q 8 3   ◊ 10 9 7 4 2
        ♣ A 2   ♣ 7 6 3
                          ♠ A 7 4
                          ♡ K J 3
                          ◊ A J 5
                          ♣ K J 8 4

Contract: 3 NT
Opening Lead: ♠ 10

Declarer played dummy's jack at trick one. East played the queen and declarer played low. He won the spade continuation and led a club. West won and played another spade setting up the spades.

Declarer, with only seven tricks, had to play a heart. West won and cashed his spades. Down one.

Question: How did declarer make 3 NT at the other table?

Better timing. She was in no rush to take the spade finesse. She won the spade opening lead with her ace and led a club. West won and continued spades.

"OK, now I'll take a finesse," thought declarer, "maybe West was leading from ♠ Q 10 9 8."

East won the queen, but the difference now was that East did not have another spade to return. Declarer now had the timing to knock out the heart ace and had plenty of tricks.

WHICH

FINESSE?

WHICH FINESSE? PERCENTAGES AND ENTRIES

The answer to this question may depend on other factors. In an excellent article in the "ACBL Bulletin," September 2016, Michael Lawrence discussed:

$$\spadesuit\ 9\ 4$$
$$\heartsuit\ 7\ 6\ 3\ 2$$
$$\diamondsuit\ A\ J\ 5\ 2$$
$$\clubsuit\ 6\ 5\ 4$$

$$\spadesuit\ A\ K$$
$$\heartsuit\ A\ Q\ 4$$
$$\diamondsuit\ K\ Q\ 10\ 9$$
$$\clubsuit\ A\ J\ 10\ 3$$

Contract: 3 NT
Opening Lead: ♠ 4

Declarer has eight sure tricks. Which suit should he finesse, hearts once or clubs twice? He doesn't have time to try both. Let's say you try a club finesse which loses and back comes another spade. OK, last chance.

Question: Another club finesse or the heart finesse?

This is a straight forward percentage play. The heart finesse is 50%. Playing on clubs twice is 75%. The clubs can be divided four ways:

West	East
♣ K Q	----
----	♣ K Q
♣ K	♣ Q
♣ Q	♣ K

Note that the double finesse will be successful in all but the first lay-out, three out of four, or 75% chance.

Entries play a role. You need two entries which you have in diamonds. With only one entry, ◊ A 5 4 3 in dummy and ◊ K Q J 6 in your hand, you have only one finesse opportunity so you should take the heart finesse, Plan B.

But with ◊ A J 4 3 and ◊ K Q 10 9, you can reach dummy twice so it's back to Plan A, clubs.

It's very annoying when both club honors are offside and the heart finesse would have been successful by taking the inferior line. The unlucky expert.

WHICH FINESSE? NOT THE OBVIOUS

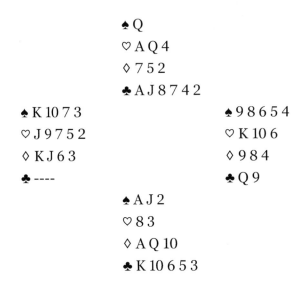

```
                          ♠ Q
                          ♡ A Q 4
                          ◇ 7 5 2
                          ♣ A J 8 7 4 2
        ♠ K 10 7 3                        ♠ 9 8 6 5 4
        ♡ J 9 7 5 2                       ♡ K 10 6
        ◇ K J 6 3                         ◇ 9 8 4
        ♣ ----                            ♣ Q 9
                          ♠ A J 2
                          ♡ 8 3
                          ◇ A Q 10
                          ♣ K 10 6 5 3
```

Contract: 5 ♣

Opening Lead: ♡ 5

It looks like there are two diamond finesses and one heart finesse. If one of three is successful, declarer will make his contract. Pretty good odds. The heart finesse at trick one lost to East's king. East returned a diamond.

Declarer lost two diamond finesses, down one.

Question: Pretty unlucky sure, but was there a better line of play?

Why are you taking all these finesses? Declarer missed the winning line at trick one. At the other table, declarer won the heart ace, led the spade queen and took a spade finesse. Where did this finesse come from you ask?

If it lost, she could discard two diamonds from dummy, losing one spade and one heart. If East covered, she could discard one diamond, losing at most one heart and take one diamond finesse later for a possible overtrick.

WHICH FINESSE? CASH ONE SUIT, FINESSE THE OTHER

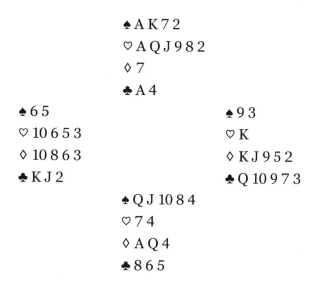

♠ A K 7 2
♡ A Q J 9 8 2
◊ 7
♣ A 4

♠ 6 5
♡ 10 6 5 3
◊ 10 8 6 3
♣ K J 2

♠ 9 3
♡ K
◊ K J 9 5 2
♣ Q 10 9 7 3

♠ Q J 10 8 4
♡ 7 4
◊ A Q 4
♣ 8 6 5

Contract: 6 ♠
Opening Lead: 2 ♣

West made a good opening lead. Declarer was faced with two choices to discard his club losers. He could finesse in hearts, hoping to set up the heart suit to discard his club losers from his hand.

Or he could take a diamond finesse to discard the one club loser in dummy.

It's a 50/50 guess. He took a heart finesse, down one.

Question: What's the general principle to follow in these situations?

It's the same as when missing two queens. Try to play for the drop in the longer suit, then finesse in the shorter suit.

At the other table, the declarer played a heart to the ace. Game, set, match.

WHICH FINESSE FIRST? SAFETY PLAY OR NOT?

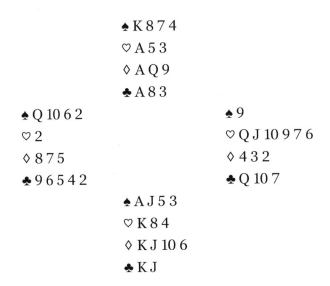

Contract: 6 NT (East opened 2 ♡)
Opening Lead: ♡ 2

At the first table, declarer ducked one round of hearts and won the heart continuation. He played a spade to the king and led a spade from dummy, planning to take a finesse. When East showed out, declarer needed a successful club finesse to hold his losses to down one.

Question: How did the other declarer make 6 NT?

Sometimes the play in one suit determines the play in another. The declarer at the other table won the opening lead in dummy and took an immediate club finesse. Why?

The best play in spades depends upon whether you have an extra club trick. When the club finesse won, declarer wanted to play the spades as safely as possible for three tricks, having nine already in the bank.

He cashed the spade ace. When East holds a singleton 9 or 10, he could continue spades, planning to cover whatever card West played to assure three spade tricks.

WHICH FINESSE AND WHY?

```
                    ♠ J 9 3
                    ♡ A K 4
                    ◊ K 2
                    ♣ A K J 10 3
    ♠ A 8 6 2                      ♠ Q 7 4
    ♡ 10 9 8 2                     ♡ 7 6 5
    ◊ Q 7                          ◊ 10 9 8 6
    ♣ 6 4 2                        ♣ 9 8 7
                    ♠ K 10 5
                    ♡ Q J 3
                    ◊ A J 5 4 3
                    ♣ Q 5
```

Contract: 6 NT
Opening Lead: ♡ 10

Declarer counted ten winners off the top. He needed two tricks and finesses were available in spades and diamonds. Where to start?

The first declarer won the opening lead in dummy and cashed the diamond king. He took a diamond finesse. You can see the result.

Question: Was this the best play?

The problem with the diamond finesse was that even if it won, declarer still needed 3-3 diamonds, or if East had four diamonds, to hold the queen of spades but not the ace.

At the other table, declarer won the opening lead and led a spade. The advantage of this play was if East had the queen, a successful finesse meant twelve tricks.

And if West won, he might not return a spade. Then the diamond play was still a backup play.

IF I MUST FINESSE, WHICH ONE?

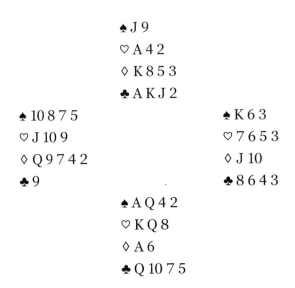

Contract: 6 NT
Opening Lead: ♡ Jack

Declarer counted his tricks, three hearts, two diamonds, and four clubs - nine in all. Needing three spade tricks, he led low to the queen, winning. He returned to dummy and led the jack. East covered with the king, ace, low. West kept his two high spades.

Down one. Had declarer started with the jack, East would have covered the first time, same result.

Question: How did declarer make 6 NT at the other table?

If you must finesse, do it properly. The best chance for three spade tricks is to take a spade finesse, but the proper one.

Declarer led low towards the ♠ J 9, hoping West had the ten. If that had lost, he would have run the jack next in case East with ♠ K 10 x forgot to cover.

This is the same way one would play needing three tricks with A J x x opposite Q 9, A 10 x x opposite K 9, or K 10 x x opposite A 9. In all of these, the best play is low to the nine.

WHICH FINESSE: TRY TO MAINTAIN TRUMP CONTROL

♠ 9 8 4
♡ 6 5 3
◊ A 10 8 4
♣ 10 9 8

♠ K Q J 7 6 3   ♠ A 10 2
♡ 10 8   ♡ 9 7 4
◊ 5 2   ◊ K 9 7 6
♣ K 7 4   ♣ 6 5 3

♠ 5
♡ A K Q J 2
◊ Q J 3
♣ A Q J 2

West	North	East	South
2♠	P	3♠	Dbl
P	4◊	P	4♡
	All Pass		

Opening Lead: ♠ King

Declarer was in a good contract, but it was not cold. Trump control might be a problem. Declarer ruffed the second spade and drew trumps, glad to see they were 3-2, first hurdle passed.

Now the minor king problems. Which one first? Declarer took a diamond finesse. East won and returned a spade. Declarer ruffed with his last trump. When the club finesse lost, West cashed all his remaining spades. Painful.

Question: What was the best way to finesse and maintain trump control?

Just an unlucky guess which way to start the minors? Not really. At the other table, after drawing trumps, declarer played ace and a club, not caring who won. He could stand one more trump force.

Now he was out of trumps, but he knew he could now take the diamond finesse into East, who he assumed, correctly, would be out of spades.

Declarer had ten tricks.

WHICH FINESSE?

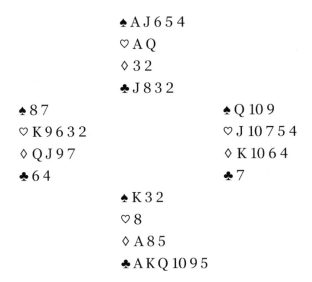

```
                        ♠ A J 6 5 4
                        ♡ A Q
                        ◇ 3 2
                        ♣ J 8 3 2
        ♠ 8 7                             ♠ Q 10 9
        ♡ K 9 6 3 2                       ♡ J 10 7 5 4
        ◇ Q J 9 7                         ◇ K 10 6 4
        ♣ 6 4                             ♣ 7
                        ♠ K 3 2
                        ♡ 8
                        ◇ A 8 5
                        ♣ A K Q 10 9 5
```

Contract: 6 ♣

Opening Lead: ◇ Queen

After the diamond lead, declarer could not afford to lose another trick. He won the opening lead and drew trumps. He cashed the spade king and led a spade to the jack. Down one.

Question: Could you have improved your chances?

The other declarer thought about taking a heart finesse. If successful, she could discard a spade from her hand and probably set up the spade suit for two diamond discards. But the spade finesse was tempting too.

So to combine all her chances when she could not afford to give up the lead, she made the best play; she didn't try either. She cashed the A-K of spades first to see if the queen would drop, about a 33% chance.

When that failed, she took the heart finesse, a combination of about 65% and was rewarded.

WHICH FINESSE? SAME PRINCIPLES

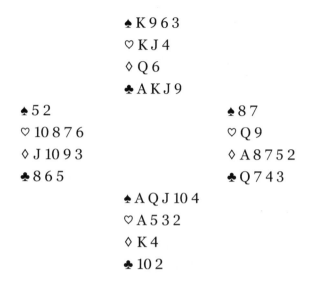

♠ K 9 6 3
♡ K J 4
◊ Q 6
♣ A K J 9

♠ 5 2
♡ 10 8 7 6
◊ J 10 9 3
♣ 8 6 5

♠ 8 7
♡ Q 9
◊ A 8 7 5 2
♣ Q 7 4 3

♠ A Q J 10 4
♡ A 5 3 2
◊ K 4
♣ 10 2

Contract: 6 ♠

Opening Lead: ◊ Jack

East won the opening lead and returned a diamond. Declarer won and drew trumps. He saw that if either the club or heart finesse was successful, he could get home.

He mentally tossed a coin and took the heart finesse. Down one.

Question: Unlucky? Get a better coin or better technique?

Unlucky yes, but at the other table, declarer applied the same principle discussed previously. When faced with two finesses, a 50-50 choice, cash the A-K of the longer suit.

So even though he was dealing with only six and seven card suits, he first cashed the A-K of the seven card heart suit.

Making six spades, no finesse necessary.

WHICH SUIT TO FINESSE

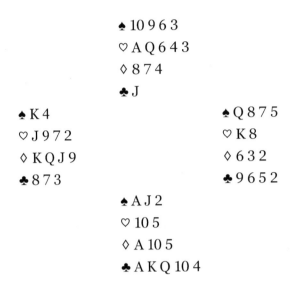

```
                  ♠ 10 9 6 3
                  ♡ A Q 6 4 3
                  ◊ 8 7 4
                  ♣ J
  ♠ K 4                           ♠ Q 8 7 5
  ♡ J 9 7 2                       ♡ K 8
  ◊ K Q J 9                       ◊ 6 3 2
  ♣ 8 7 3                         ♣ 9 6 5 2
                  ♠ A J 2
                  ♡ 10 5
                  ◊ A 10 5
                  ♣ A K Q 10 4
```

Contract: 3 NT
Opening Lead: ◊ King

Declarer won the third round of diamonds, East following to all three rounds. With eight sure tricks, declarer took a heart finesse. He finished with the same eight tricks he started with. Down one.

Question: Was there a better line of play for that elusive ninth trick?

The other declarer knew some basic odds. The heart finesse was 50%. But since West had only one more diamond to cash, there was another line of play that was 75%. He could take two spade finesses, playing for split spade honors or both spade honors with East.

At trick four he played a club to dummy's jack and took a spade finesse. West won the king and cashed his last club. Now West played a heart. Staying with his original plan, declarer went up with the ace and took another spade finesse.

Making nine tricks. Scary but the right play. As Mike Lawrence would probably say, if West had both spade honors and the heart finesse would have worked, go read someone else's book.

WHICH FINESSE: FIRST THE ONE YOU DON'T "NEED"

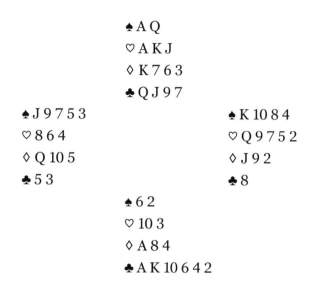

♠ A Q
♥ A K J
♦ K 7 6 3
♣ Q J 9 7

♠ J 9 7 5 3
♥ 8 6 4
♦ Q 10 5
♣ 5 3

♠ K 10 8 4
♥ Q 9 7 5 2
♦ J 9 2
♣ 8

♠ 6 2
♥ 10 3
♦ A 8 4
♣ A K 10 6 4 2

Contract: 6 ♣

Opening Lead: ♣ 3

Declarer drew trumps and took a spade finesse. East won the king and returned a spade. With an unavoidable diamond loser, now declarer tried a heart finesse. Down one.

Question: Was there a better way to combine all your chances?

Think hand type. Sometimes a second suit is there, but like a good woman, is hard to find. To combine his chances, the declarer at the other table took a heart finesse first, seemingly a finesse he did not need.

But now he threw his diamond loser on the good heart in dummy. When diamonds divided 3-3, he did not need the spade finesse. If that plan had failed, the spade finesse could be a LAST RESORT.

31

WHICH FINESSE: ONE CHANCE

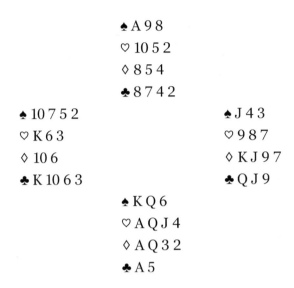

♠ A 9 8
♡ 10 5 2
◊ 8 5 4
♣ 8 7 4 2

♠ 10 7 5 2
♡ K 6 3
◊ 10 6
♣ K 10 6 3

♠ J 4 3
♡ 9 8 7
◊ K J 9 7
♣ Q J 9

♠ K Q 6
♡ A Q J 4
◊ A Q 3 2
♣ A 5

Contract: 3 NT
Opening Lead: ♣ 3

East played the jack at trick one and declarer won his ace. With only one dummy entry, he had to decide which red suit to finesse. It seemed like a 50-50 choice. He went to dummy and led the ten of hearts to finesse.

West won the king. The defense cashed three rounds of clubs and exited a spade. Declarer lost a diamond trick at the end. Down one.

Question: Was there any reason to try one finesse over the other?

Declarer had three heart tricks on power. Leading the heart ten would gain if East held K x x. But if East held K x or K 9 8 x, declarer would still win only three heart tricks.

A winning diamond finesse however, would be a sure ninth trick. The other declarer led a diamond to his queen at trick three. Nine tricks.

WHICH ONE FIRST?

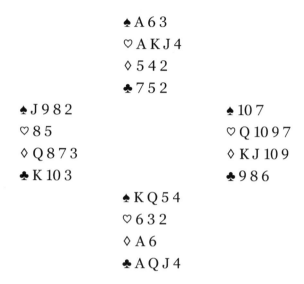

Contract: 3 NT

Opening Lead: ♠ 2

Declarer won the queen of spades and led a heart to the jack. East won the queen and shifted to diamonds. Declarer won his ace and tried a club finesse. When that lost, the defense cashed three diamond tricks. Down one.

"Zero for two," lamented South. North was muttering under his breath.

Question: Can you imagine what North was thinking? Feeling sorry for South?

At the other table, declarer did things the other way around. He saw that if he finessed first in hearts and lost, he would need the club finesse.

But if he took a club finesse first and lost, he might have nine tricks without resorting to a heart finesse. So he took the club finesse. Bad news, it lost. Good news, clubs were 3-3. Nine tricks, no heart finesse.

SAME PRINCIPLE, A DIFFERENT SCENE

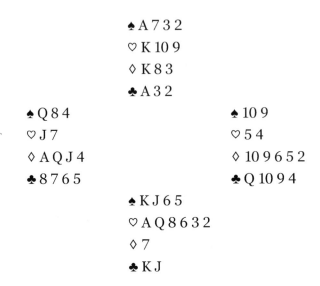

Contract: 6 ♡

Opening Lead: ◊ Ace

West led the ace, then queen of diamonds, declarer discarding a spade on the diamond king. After drawing trumps, declarer took a losing spade finesse, down one.

"My finesses never win," complained South. "Didn't you read Dr J's book," asked North?

Question: What was North referring to? How should South have played?

The other declarer, in an attempt to combine his chances, saw more than one possible finesse. After drawing trumps, he cashed the A-K of spades, his longer suit. When the queen didn't fall, he took a club finesse.

When the jack won, he cashed the club king, and threw his remaining spade loser on the club ace. It's the same principle of two finesses; cash the longer, finesse the shorter.

YOUR CHOICE: ABOUT 36% OR 75%

```
                        ♠ 7 3 2
                        ♡ 10 8 2
                        ◊ A Q 5 3 2
                        ♣ 6 2
        ♠ Q J 10 4                    ♠ K 8 6
        ♡ K 5                         ♡ Q 7 6 4
        ◊ 10 9 7 6                    ◊ 8 4
        ♣ 10 7 4                      ♣ J 9 8 3
                        ♠ A 9 5
                        ♡ A J 9 3
                        ◊ K J
                        ♣ A K Q 5
```

Contract: 3 NT

Opening Lead: ♠ Queen

Declarer won the third round of spades. He cashed the diamond king, then played the diamond jack and overtook with the ace. When he cashed the diamond queen, East showed out. Shocking!

Declarer tried to recover, playing the heart ten, but West won his king, cashed a diamond and spade for down one.

Question: The odds of a suit being 3-3 are about 36%. How should South play?

The other declarer took a more realistic view. There was a 75% play available that we have discussed. Play for split heart honors, using the diamonds as entries.

He used the diamonds as entries to take two heart finesses. This declarer took one spade, three hearts, three clubs, and two diamonds.

TWO CHANCES ARE BETTER THAN ONE

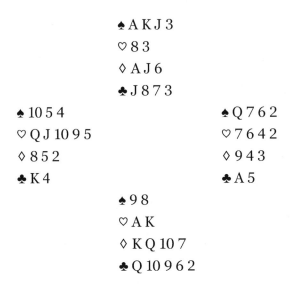

```
                    ♠ A K J 3
                    ♡ 8 3
                    ◇ A J 6
                    ♣ J 8 7 3
   ♠ 10 5 4                          ♠ Q 7 6 2
   ♡ Q J 10 9 5                      ♡ 7 6 4 2
   ◇ 8 5 2                           ◇ 9 4 3
   ♣ K 4                             ♣ A 5
                    ♠ 9 8
                    ♡ A K
                    ◇ K Q 10 7
                    ♣ Q 10 9 6 2
```

Contract: 3 NT

Opening Lead: ♡ Queen

Declarer had a lot of tricks, eleven in all. But three no trump, or any number of no trump, is a race. In this case, could declarer win nine before the defenders win five? And the defenders had a head start. If declarer tried to develop clubs, he would lose the race.

So he had to look elsewhere for the ninth trick. Spades was the obvious suit. Declarer played a spade to the jack, losing to East's queen. A heart came back. Declarer cashed the A-K spades, but still had only eight tricks. The last spade was not high.

Question: Anybody see a ninth trick anywhere?

The other declarer saw a chance for two finesses, not just one. At trick two, she led the spade nine, but played low from dummy, not the jack. If this lost to the ten, she could try again the next time. But now she had a ninth trick.

THREE FINESSES? ONE IS ENOUGH

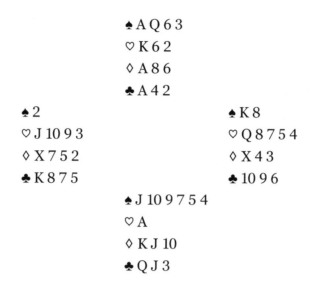

```
                    ♠ A Q 6 3
                    ♡ K 6 2
                    ◊ A 8 6
                    ♣ A 4 2
    ♠ 2                          ♠ K 8
    ♡ J 10 9 3                   ♡ Q 8 7 5 4
    ◊ X 7 5 2                    ◊ X 4 3
    ♣ K 8 7 5                    ♣ 10 9 6
                    ♠ J 10 9 7 5 4
                    ♡ A
                    ◊ K J 10
                    ♣ Q J 3
```

Contract: 6 ♠

Opening Lead: ♡ Jack

Declarer won the opening lead and took a trump finesse. East won and returned a trump. Declarer took a successful club finesse and discarded one club on the heart king. He now had to guess the diamonds, a two-way guess. Down one.

Question: This declarer was one out of three. Could you have done better?

The first declarer's batting average was one out of three. Why so many finesses? Before starting the trumps, the other declarer took the club finesse, winning.

After West covered the first or second club, declarer discarded her remaining club on the heart king and ruffed dummy's last heart.

She cashed the ace of trumps, no finesse, thank you, and ruffed dummy's last club. She played a trump. Whoever won the spade king had to break the diamond suit.

One finesse only, making six spades.

WHICH FINESSE OR FINESSES?

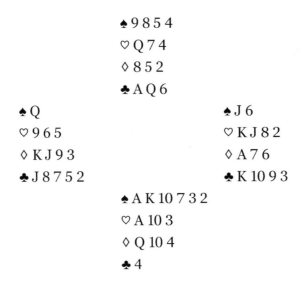

Contract: 3 ♠

Opening Lead: ♢ 3

The defense took the first three diamond tricks. At trick four, West led the five of clubs. Declarer, a finesse addict, took the finesse and created an extra loser. Down two.

Question: Think about some basic percentage plays. What would you do?

The club finesse was a 50% play. If it won, declarer could discard one heart loser. Fine. If it lost, he had created an extra loser.

In the heart suit, declarer had a 75% chance to make his contract without adding an extra loser.

One approach was to play the ace of hearts and lead to the queen, also a 50% play. But there is a BIG card, the ten. The other declarer made the best play, low to the queen of hearts first.

If that finesse had lost to the king, he could still lead towards the ♡ A 10 and finesse the ♡ J, a 75% chance without creating an extra loser.

TWO EQUAL FINESSES: CASH ONE. FINESSE THE OTHER

```
                      ♠ J 4
                      ♡ K 9 5 3
                      ◊ K 8 4
                      ♣ A J 10 2
        ♠ Q 10 6 2                      ♠ K 8 7 5 3
        ♡ Q 6                           ♡ 10 8 7
        ◊ J 9 6 5                       ◊ 3
        ♣ 9 8 3                         ♣ K 7 6 4
                      ♠ A 9
                      ♡ A J 4 2
                      ◊ A Q 10 7 2
                      ♣ Q 5
```

Contract: 3 NT
Opening Lead: ♠ 2

Declarer tried the jack at trick one. East played the king and declarer won the ace. Declarer counted nine tricks, even if East had four diamonds. But play slowed when East showed out on the second diamond.

Searching for tricks, declarer took a club finesse. East won and the defense cashed four spade tricks. Down one.

Question: Unlucky or poor declarer technique?

The other declarer, faced with the same problem of finding tricks elsewhere, saw two suits as a possible source of tricks. With nothing to go on, she decided to cash the high honors in the suit in which she had the most cards.

If nothing good happened, she planned on finessing in the other suit.

When the A-K of hearts dropped the queen, declarer had nine tricks, no finesse needed, thank you.

WHICH FINESSE TO TAKE? NONE, REALLY

$\spadesuit$ J 4
$\heartsuit$ K 7 5 2
$\diamondsuit$ J 5
$\clubsuit$ A Q J 10 8

$\spadesuit$ 10 9 8 3 $\spadesuit$ K Q 7 6 5
$\heartsuit$ J $\heartsuit$ 10 8
$\diamondsuit$ X 8 7 3 $\diamondsuit$ X 6 2
$\clubsuit$ X 7 4 2 $\clubsuit$ X 5 3

$\spadesuit$ A 2
$\heartsuit$ A Q 9 6 4 3
$\diamondsuit$ A Q 10 4
$\clubsuit$ 9

Contract: 6 $\heartsuit$

Opening Lead: $\spadesuit$ 10

The spade lead made the contract difficult. With any other lead, the slam was cold. At one table, declarer looked at the two finesse possibilities. If either was successful, he could discard a spade loser from either hand.

After drawing trumps, he took one of the finesses. It lost, down one. North just shook his head. You could almost see the tears.

Question: Why was North ready to find a new partner?

Instead of trying to guess which, if either finesse to take, the other declarer simply played a club to the ace and led the club queen. It didn't matter who had the club king. A simple ruffing finesse was coming.

If East had the club king and covered, South would ruff and the clubs were good. If East didn't cover, declarer would discard her spade loser.

If West had the club king, declarer would have the rest of the tricks.

WHICH FINESSE? NO FINESSE

```
                        ♠ 8 6 4
                        ♡ A 10 6 2
                        ◊ K 6 3
                        ♣ 10 5 4
        ♠ K J 3                         ♠ Q 9 7 5
        ♡ 3                             ♡ K 5
        ◊ Q 10 7                        ◊ 9 8 5 4 2
        ♣ K Q 9 8 6 2                   ♣ 7 3
                        ♠ A 10 2
                        ♡ Q J 9 8 7 4
                        ◊ A J
                        ♣ A J
```

South	West	North	East
1 ♡	2 ♣	2 ♡	P
4 ♡		All Pass	

Opening Lead: ♣ King

Declarer won the club ace. He led the heart queen and took a finesse. East won and returned a club. West won and played another club. East ruffed and declarer overruffed. But he still had more two losers, no matter how he proceeded, down one.

Question: Having avoided a spade lead, how should declarer play?

Again timing, NO finesses. Instead of taking a trump finesse, the other declarer played the ace. Hey, on a good day, missing only three the king might fall. OK, no king.

But now declarer played another club himself, establishing the club ten in dummy for a spade discard. The diamond king was his entry.

WHICH FINESSE?

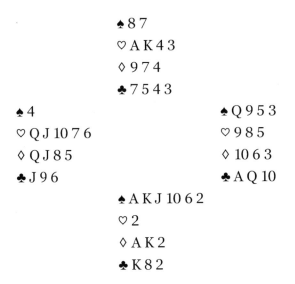

♠ 8 7
♥ A K 4 3
⋄ 9 7 4
♣ 7 5 4 3

♠ 4
♥ Q J 10 7 6
⋄ Q J 8 5
♣ J 9 6

♠ Q 9 5 3
♥ 9 8 5
⋄ 10 6 3
♣ A Q 10

♠ A K J 10 6 2
♥ 2
⋄ A K 2
♣ K 8 2

Contract: 4 ♠
Opening Lead: ♥ Queen

Declarer won the heart ace, cashed the heart king, discarding a diamond and took a trump finesse. It won, but when he played the A-K of trumps next, the queen was still out.

Since he could not reach the dummy, he also lost three club tricks, down one.

Question: How should declarer make use of his one time in dummy?

A successful club finesse would guarantee the contract. And if it lost, there was still the possibility of dropping the trump queen under the A-K. On the other hand, one successful trump finesse might not be enough.

So the other declarer used his one appearance in the dummy to lead a club towards his king. Ten tricks.

WHICH FINESSE FIRST? ONLY ONE?

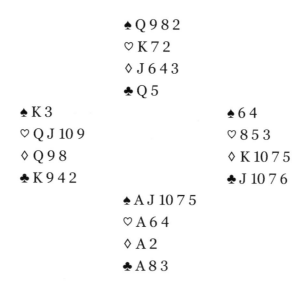

```
                    ♠ Q 9 8 2
                    ♡ K 7 2
                    ◇ J 6 4 3
                    ♣ Q 5
      ♠ K 3                          ♠ 6 4
      ♡ Q J 10 9                     ♡ 8 5 3
      ◇ Q 9 8                        ◇ K 10 7 5
      ♣ K 9 4 2                      ♣ J 10 7 6
                    ♠ A J 10 7 5
                    ♡ A 6 4
                    ◇ A 2
                    ♣ A 8 3
```

Contract: 4 ♠
Opening Lead: ♡ Queen

There is a potential loser in each suit. Declarer won the opening lead in dummy and took a spade finesse, losing to West's king. Back came the heart jack. The one loser in each suit came true. Down one.

Question: Overbid or poor planning?

There is another finesse, a bit obscure, but one that if timed properly gives declarer a chance to make his contract.

The slow heart might be avoided. The other declarer won the opening lead in hand and led a low club. If West had the king and ducked, no club loser. If he won and continued hearts, he would win in dummy.

Declarer would then cash the club queen, come to the diamond ace and play the club ace discarding the heart loser. If East had the club king, he was no worse off, but at least would have made an effort.

Now ruff the heart and take the trump finesse for a possible overtrick.

WHICH FINESSE FIRST? COUNT YOUR TRICKS

$$\spadesuit\ 7\ 6$$
$$\heartsuit\ A\ J\ 4$$
$$\diamond\ K\ J\ 5\ 2$$
$$\clubsuit\ 7\ 6\ 5\ 4$$

$\spadesuit$ Q J 10 5 3 $\spadesuit$ 9 8 4
$\heartsuit$ K 9 8 $\heartsuit$ 7 6 5 3
$\diamond$ 10 8 7 6 $\diamond$ Q 9
$\clubsuit$ Q $\clubsuit$ K J 10 9

$$\spadesuit\ A\ K\ 2$$
$$\heartsuit\ Q\ 10\ 2$$
$$\diamond\ A\ 4\ 3$$
$$\clubsuit\ A\ 8\ 3\ 2$$

Contract: 3 NT
Opening Lead: $\spadesuit$ Queen

Declarer won the opening lead and played the ace of diamonds. He played a diamond to the jack, losing to East's queen. East returned a spade.

The heart finesse won but when the diamonds split 4-2, declarer only had eight tricks. Down one.

Question: Unlucky or poorly planned?

Often the play in one suit depends upon another suit. Declarer doesn't know how many diamond tricks she needs until she plays the heart suit. At the other table, the declarer took a heart finesse at trick two.

Had the heart finesse lost, declarer would need four diamond tricks and need to play West for $\diamond$ Q x x. But needing only three diamond tricks, the other declarer played as safely as possible, by playing the A-K of diamonds before leading towards the jack.

She was rewarded when the queen fell.

WHICH FINESSE? A TWO - FOR - ONE SPECIAL

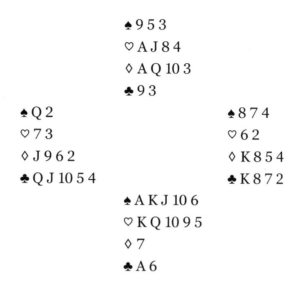

```
                    ♠ 9 5 3
                    ♡ A J 8 4
                    ♢ A Q 10 3
                    ♣ 9 3
      ♠ Q 2                        ♠ 8 7 4
      ♡ 7 3                        ♡ 6 2
      ♢ J 9 6 2                    ♢ K 8 5 4
      ♣ Q J 10 5 4                 ♣ K 8 7 2
                    ♠ A K J 10 6
                    ♡ K Q 10 9 5
                    ♢ 7
                    ♣ A 6
```

Contract: 6 ♡

Opening Lead: ♣ Queen

Declarer won the opening lead and drew trumps. He had two options to discard his club loser: take a spade finesse, the percentage play in spades, or take a diamond finesse.

If either loses, the defense will cash a club. Declarer chose_____. Down one.

Question: Which would you have chosen (Yes, I know you can see all 4 hands).

This is a classic two for one special. It's a complete guess which to choose, so cash the high honors from the long suit, spades, first. If nothing good happens, finesse in the other suit, diamonds. A two – for – one.

WHICH FIRST? ONE MORE TWO - FOR - ONE

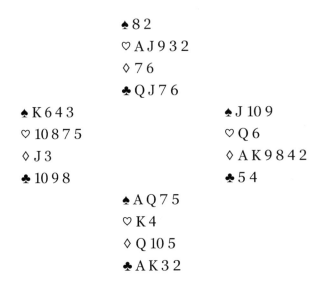

Contract: 3 NT (East bid diamonds)
Opening Lead: ◊ Jack

East ducked the first trick to keep communication. Declarer had eight tricks. A ninth trick could come from a heart or spade finesse. It's a 50-50 chance.

One declarer took a heart finesse. Lots of undertricks, too many to count.

Question: What's the best play for nine tricks?

It's another two -for -one special. Since either finesse could be right (or wrong), cash the high ones in your long suit (hearts), then if nothing good has happened, take a finesse in the other suit (spades).

The other declarer, after winning the first trick with the diamond queen, cashed the A-K of hearts. One spade, three hearts, one diamond, and four clubs.

WHICH FINESSE FIRST? THE ONE
THAT KEEPS YOU ALIVE

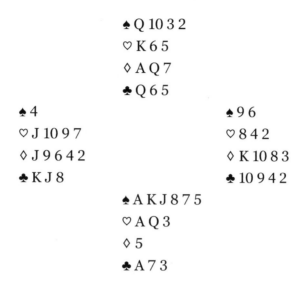

♠ Q 10 3 2
♡ K 6 5
◊ A Q 7
♣ Q 6 5

♠ 4
♡ J 10 9 7
◊ J 9 6 4 2
♣ K J 8

♠ 9 6
♡ 8 4 2
◊ K 10 8 3
♣ 10 9 4 2

♠ A K J 8 7 5
♡ A Q 3
◊ 5
♣ A 7 3

Contract: 6 ♠

Opening Lead: ♡ Jack

Declarer has eleven top tricks. He needed either a successful diamond finesse or the club king with West. Declarer took a diamond finesse, losing to East's king. After much agonizing, he ended with eleven tricks.

Question. How would you have played this slam?

When faced with two finesses, needing only one to succeed, always first try the one that if it loses, you are still in the game. If you try the diamond finesse first and it loses, you are down even if the club finesse succeeds.

If you try the club finesse first and it loses, you are still alive to try the diamond finesse. So after drawing trumps, lead a low club. You have a 75% chance of making this slam, needing one of two finesses to succeed.

IF I MUST FINESSE, WHICH ONE FIRST?

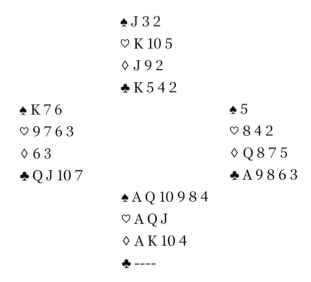

```
                    ♠ J 3 2
                    ♡ K 10 5
                    ◇ J 9 2
                    ♣ K 5 4 2
♠ K 7 6                              ♠ 5
♡ 9 7 6 3                            ♡ 8 4 2
◇ 6 3                                ◇ Q 8 7 5
♣ Q J 10 7                           ♣ A 9 8 6 3
                    ♠ A Q 10 9 8 4
                    ♡ A Q J
                    ◇ A K 10 4
                    ♣ ----
```

Contract: 6 ♠

Opening Lead: ♣ Queen

Declarer ruffed the opening lead and was faced with a choice of two finesses, but only one dummy entry. Which finesse to take?

She went to dummy with a heart and led the trump jack, losing. She could not take the diamond finesse. Even if she had led a low trump to her queen, West could play low effectively. Down one.

Question: Which finesse should declarer take first and why?

Always try to take the one that if it fails, you are not down (yet). At the other table, declarer went to dummy and led the diamond nine.

If it had lost, the jack of diamonds was now an entry for a trump finesse.

TWO FINESSES, PICK WHICH ONE

```
                    ♠ 2
                    ♡ 8
                    ◇ A K J 10 7 6
                    ♣ A J 9 5 4
        ♠ Q 9 5                      ♠ 10 8 7 4
        ♡ A K 7 6 5 2                ♡ 10 9 3
        ◇ 9 8 5                      ◇ Q 4
        ♣ 2                          ♣ K 8 6 3
                    ♠ A K J 6 3
                    ♡ Q J 4
                    ◇ 3 2
                    ♣ Q 10 7
```

North	East	South	West
1 ◇	P	1 ♠	2 ♡
3 ♣	P	3 NT	All Pass

Opening Lead: ♡ 6

Declarer won the opening lead and needed the next eight tricks. Faced with two sources of tricks, one missing a king, one missing a queen, where to start?

The first declarer took a diamond finesse. Painful.

Question: What general principle should one follow here?

Quoting Eddie Kantar: "Remember your 'combining' rule and stay alive, stay alive!" It sounds like the Bee Gees song "Staying Alive, Staying alive."

At the other table, the declarer followed Eddie's (and the Bee Gees) advice.

When you have two finesse suits, one missing a king, the other a queen, and either provides enough tricks to make your contract, first cash the A-K of the suit missing the queen.

If nothing good happens, take a finesse in the other suit for the king.

Making 3 NT

49

WHICH FINESSE FOR WHAT?

```
                    ♠ K 7 3
                    ♡ 4 2
                    ◊ K J 9 4
                    ♣ A 10 9 3
        ♠ 10 9 4 2                    ♠ J 8 6
        ♡ 10 7                        ♡ K J 9 8 6 3
        ◊ Q 7 6 2                     ◊ A 5
        ♣ 8 5 2                       ♣ K 4
                    ♠ A Q 5
                    ♡ A Q 5
                    ◊ 10 8 3
                    ♣ Q J 7 6
```

North	East	South	West
P	1 ♡	1 NT	P
3 NT		All Pass	

Opening Lead: ♡ 10

Declarer won the first trick with the heart queen and took a club finesse. East won and returned a heart. Declarer only had eight tricks before East got in with the diamond ace. Down one.

Question: Was that the best finesse?

East was a big favorite to hold the diamond ace, and most likely the club king. The only card that might be up for grabs is the diamond queen. After winning the heart queen, the other declarer led the diamond eight and let it ride.

East won the ace and continued hearts, but declarer repeated the diamond finesse and 3 NT was coming home.

She won three diamonds, two hearts, three spades, and at least one club, probably two on an endplay.

WHICH FINESSE? THE SAME PRINCIPLE

```
                      ♠ A K J 8
                      ♡ 8
                      ◊ A J 10
                      ♣ Q 9 8 6 2
        ♠ 7 6 4 3                        ♠ Q 2
        ♡ 5 2                            ♡ A Q J 10 9 4
        ◊ 7 6 4 2                        ◊ K 8 5 3
        ♣ 7 4 3                          ♣ 5
                      ♠ 10 9 5
                      ♡ K 7 6 3
                      ◊ Q 9
                      ♣ A K J 10
```

South	West	North	East
1 ♣	P	1 ♠	2 ♡
Dbl*	P	3 ♡	P	* 3 Spades
3 NT	P	4 ♣	P
5 ♣	P	6 ♣	All Pass

Opening Lead: ♡ 5

East won the first trick and returned a trump. Declarer saw that a winning diamond or spade finesse would bring home this slam, providing a discard for the loser in the other suit. He mentally elected one and went down.

It actually didn't matter which one if he was electing to finesse first.

Question: Since both finesses will lose, what should declarer have done?

We have seen this principle with two long suits; cash the longest first. If nothing good happens, take a finesse in the other suit.

The other declarer realized this was the same principle, just with shorter suits. When it's a 50-50 guess, cash the longer of the two first, then finesse the other if necessary. So in this case, cash the spades. Voila! Hey, you are entitled to a little good luck once in awhile.

LOTS OF FINESSES: WHERE TO START?

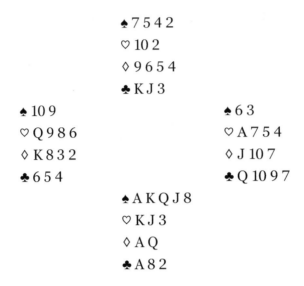

```
                        ♠ 7 5 4 2
                        ♡ 10 2
                        ◊ 9 6 5 4
                        ♣ K J 3
        ♠ 10 9                          ♠ 6 3
        ♡ Q 9 8 6                       ♡ A 7 5 4
        ◊ K 8 3 2                       ◊ J 10 7
        ♣ 6 5 4                         ♣ Q 10 9 7
                        ♠ A K Q J 8
                        ♡ K J 3
                        ◊ A Q
                        ♣ A 8 2
```

Contract: 4 ♠

Opening Lead: ♠ 10

Declarer won the opening lead and drew trumps. Being a finesse addict, he couldn't wait to get started. He took a losing club finesse, a losing diamond finesse, and topped it off by leading a heart towards his hand and misguessing.

Down one. "Don't start complaining to me about your bad luck," said North.

Question: Was North second guessing him or was there a better line of play?

The other declarer didn't want to take any finesses until forced. She drew trumps and saw a card of value the other declarer overlooked. Do you see it?

The ten of hearts. She led a heart. It could have been low to the ten, or even the king first. But she had the timing to set up a heart trick for a club discard. A diamond came back, and she lost that finesse.

But she won the race to ten tricks

FINESSE? OK BUT WHICH ONES?

```
                    ♠ Q J 9 3
                    ♡ Q 9 3
                    ◊ J 9 3
                    ♣ Q 9 3
    ♠ 10 6 4 2                      ♠ 8 7 5
    ♡ K 8                           ♡ 2
    ◊ K 8 6                         ◊ 10 7 5 4 2
    ♣ J 10 8 7                      ♣ A 6 5 2
                    ♠ A K
                    ♡ A J 10 7 6 5 4
                    ◊ A Q
                    ♣ K 4
```

South	West	North	East
2 ♣	P	2 ◊	P
2 ♡	P	3 ♡	P
4 NT	P	5 ◊	P
5 ♡		All Pass	

Opening Lead: ♣ Jack

Declarer played low, East played the ace, declarer played low. East returned a diamond. Declarer, having had his finesses lose all day, hopefully played the queen, West won the king. West's later trump trick meant down one.

Question: Was there any road to five hearts?

At the other table, the declarer was playing against two experts. Knowing declarer was missing two key cards, if East had the club ten, ♣ A 10 x (x), he would have ducked trick one. He knew his partner had an entry. Another club from West would give him a chance for two club tricks.

So declarer unblocked his club king under the ace. He won the diamond return with the ace, no finesse, and took his own finesse, a club towards dummy's ♣ Q 9 to discard his diamond loser.

SECOND
SUITS

NO FINESSE: BASIC SECOND SUIT PLAY

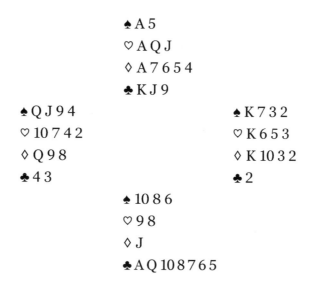

♠ A 5
♡ A Q J
◇ A 7 6 5 4
♣ K J 9

♠ Q J 9 4
♡ 10 7 4 2
◇ Q 9 8
♣ 4 3

♠ K 7 3 2
♡ K 6 5 3
◇ K 10 3 2
♣ 2

♠ 10 8 6
♡ 9 8
◇ J
♣ A Q 10 8 7 6 5

Contract: 6 ♣

Opening Lead: ♠ Queen

Declarer won the opening lead and drew trumps. He took a heart finesse. East won and cashed a spade. Down one. Sure, swift, and wrong.

Question: Could you have improved the odds from declarer's 50% play?

At least that was quick. The other declarer was in no hurry to try the finesse. Setting up the diamond suit offered better odds, and if diamonds broke 5-2, or trumps broke 3-0, he had the heart finesse as Plan B.

He cashed the ace of diamonds, diamond ruff, a trump to dummy, and a diamond ruff. Now another trump to dummy and another diamond ruff. The heart ace was the entry to the good diamond.

He discarded a heart on the diamond, conceded a spade, and ruffed his last spade with dummy's last trump.

TWO TEMPTING FINESSES: NEITHER, A SECOND SUIT

```
                          ♠ A Q
                          ♡ K Q 2
                          ◊ 8 6 4 3 2
                          ♣ 8 5 2
        ♠ J 9 6 3 2                        ♠ K 10 7 5
        ♡ 4                                ♡ 9 8 3
        ◊ K J 9 7                          ◊ 10 5
        ♣ 10 9 6                           ♣ A K Q J
                          ♠ 8 4
                          ♡ A J 10 7 6 5
                          ◊ A Q
                          ♣ 7 4 3
```

East	South	West	North
1♣	1♡	P	2♣
P	2♡	P	3♡
	All Pass		

Opening Lead: ♣ 10

East cashed three rounds of clubs and switched to a diamond. Declarer played the queen. West won the king and shifted to a spade. Declarer knew that finesse would lose since East had opened the bidding.

He won the ace and played the diamond ace. He led a trump to dummy and ruffed a diamond. But when the suit was 4-2, declarer was down one.

Question: Unlucky, mistimed, any better ideas?

The other declarer also saw a second suit but realized entries were a problem. How would you play if your diamonds were ◊ A 2? The queen was a 'mirage'. You would win the ace of diamonds, then play the two. He rejected the diamond finesse, won the ace and played the queen of diamonds.

Now he was a step ahead. He won the spade return, no finesse, ruffed a diamond, led a trump to dummy and ruffed another diamond. He drew trumps ending in the dummy. The spade loser went on the fifth diamond.

FINESSE OR SECOND SUIT

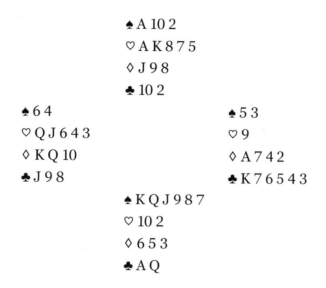

♠ A 10 2
♡ A K 8 7 5
◇ J 9 8
♣ 10 2

♠ 6 4
♡ Q J 6 4 3
◇ K Q 10
♣ J 9 8

♠ 5 3
♡ 9
◇ A 7 4 2
♣ K 7 6 5 4 3

♠ K Q J 9 8 7
♡ 10 2
◇ 6 5 3
♣ A Q

Contract: 4 ♠
Opening Lead: ◇ King

East led the diamond king, continued with the queen, then the ten to East's ace. East returned a low club. Declarer, having bought my book about finesses, saw the club finesse was 50%, but setting up the hearts to discard the clubs was about 84%.

She won the club ace, cashed one high spade from her hand, leaving two trump entries in dummy, and then played the A-K of hearts, planning to ruff a heart. She could return with a spade to ruff another heart, if necessary.

Question: What was the result? What happened at the other table?

The other declarer had not bought my book. He took a club finesse.
Eddie Kantar showed me this hand at a NABC a few years ago. I quote Eddie:
"What happened? East ruffed the second heart and cashed the club king. The club finesse was onside. Why am I so mean? I'm not. You played the hand properly." Yes, rejecting the club finesse in favor of a second suit was best.

Eddie said "Only someone who misplayed the hand and took the club finesse made it. For shame if you made this hand!"

NO FINESSE NEEDED, 100% PLAY INSTEAD

                          ♠ K 6 2
                          ♡ 7 5 3
                          ◊ 10 9 7 4
                          ♣ A 6 5
        ♠ J 10 9 7 3   ♠ 8 4
        ♡ J   ♡ Q 10 9 8 6
        ◊ K 3   ◊ J 8 6 5 2
        ♣ J 10 8 7 3   ♣ Q
                          ♠ A Q 5
                          ♡ A K 4 2
                          ◊ A Q
                          ♣ K 9 4 2

Contract: 3 NT
Opening Lead: ♠ Jack

Declarer counted eight winners. He tried for a 3-3 split in clubs or hearts, and when neither suit behaved, took a diamond finesse. Down one.

"Pretty unlucky," moaned South. "I must have been about an 80% favorite to make." "Too bad you didn't take the 100% play," replied North.

Question: What was North referring to?

At the other table, declarer also saw eight winners, but knew he had a sure ninth trick in diamonds. At trick two, he played the ace, then queen of diamonds.

With two dummy entries, he was assured of another diamond trick for his ninth trick with the remaining ◊ 10 9 in the dummy.

SECOND SUIT BUT NO FINESSES

```
                    ♠ A Q 6 4 2
                    ♡ K 8 7
                    ◊ 5 3
                    ♣ 8 6 2
        ♠ J 9 8 5                      ♠ K 10
        ♡ 6 4 3                        ♡ 5 2
        ◊ J 9 6 2                      ◊ K Q 10 7 4
        ♣ J 3                          ♣ K Q 10 9
                    ♠ 7 3
                    ♡ A Q J 10 9
                    ◊ A 8
                    ♣ A 7 5 4
```

East	South	West	North
1 ◊	1 ♡	P	2 ♡
P	4 ♡	All Pass	

Opening Lead: ◊ 2

Declarer won the opening lead, and started setting up the spades by playing low to the queen. East won the king, cashed a diamond, and shifted to a trump.

Declarer won, cashed the spade ace and ruffed a spade, but when he saw East discard, was lucky to go down only one.

Question: Wrong game plan or what?

Right game plan, wrong execution, perhaps self - execution. A second suit hand but entry problems. The spade finesse was sure to lose from the bidding. At trick two, the other declarer played a low spade from both hands.

East won, cashed a diamond and led the club king. Declarer won the ace, played a spade to the ace and ruffed a spade. He drew trumps ending in the dummy and cashed the good spades.

SOME SECOND SUITS ARE HARD TO FIND

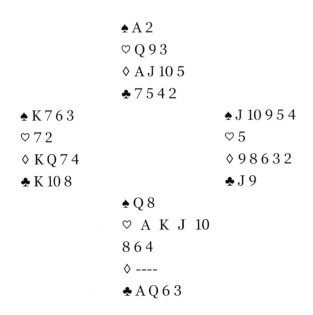

♠ A 2
♡ Q 9 3
◊ A J 10 5
♣ 7 5 4 2

♠ K 7 6 3　　　　　　　　♠ J 10 9 5 4
♡ 7 2　　　　　　　　　　♡ 5
◊ K Q 7 4　　　　　　　　◊ 9 8 6 3 2
♣ K 10 8　　　　　　　　 ♣ J 9

♠ Q 8
♡ A K J 10
8 6 4
◊ ----
♣ A Q 6 3

Contract:　6 ♡

Opening Lead:　◊ King

Declarer won the opening lead, discarding a club and played the diamond jack, discarding another club. West won and played a trump. Declarer drew trumps, discarded the spade loser on the high diamond, and took a club finesse. Down one.

Question: Could you have taken advantage of the helpful, ill-judged lead?

At the other table, declarer thought about hand type. Second suit? Maybe. Play started the same the first two tricks, but when declarer won the trump return at trick three, he won in hand and cashed the club ace. He led a trump to dummy and discarded his last club on the high diamond.

He ruffed a club, both opponents followed. Another trump to dummy was followed by another club ruff. The spade ace was the entry to the good club, to use for a spade discard. Sometimes a second suit is hard to find.

NO FINESSE: A SECOND SUIT

$$\spadesuit\ A K J 5$$
$$\heartsuit\ A J 7 5 3$$
$$\diamond\ 2$$
$$\clubsuit\ K 9 7$$

♠ 4 3	♠ Q 10 8 7
♡ K 9 4	♡ Q 10 6 2
◊ A Q 8 7 5 3	◊ 10 9 6 4
♣ 6 3	♣ 10

$$\spadesuit\ 9 6 2$$
$$\heartsuit\ 8$$
$$\diamond\ K J$$
$$\clubsuit\ A Q J 8 5 4 2$$

West	North	East	South
2 ◊	Dbl	4 ◊	5 ♣
3 NT	6 ♣	All Pass	

Opening Lead: ◊ Ace

The opening lead did not help declarer very much. West switched to the spade four. Declarer won the ace, drew trumps and took a spade finesse. Down one.

Question: Was there a better line of play?

Maybe. If one line of play doesn't work, the finesse can be a LAST RESORT. The other declarer decided to try to set up the heart suit. Timing was critical to have a late entry.

He won the spade ace and played a club to his ace. He played a heart to the ace, ruffed a heart high, a trump to dummy, and another heart ruff. The hearts were dividing 4-3.

Another trump to dummy, and one more heart ruff established the last heart. The spade king was the entry. The losing spade went on the last heart.

NO FINESSES: SECOND SUIT

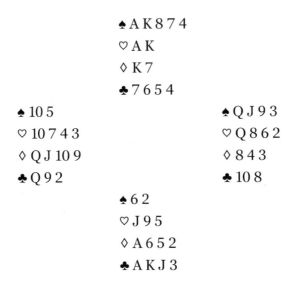

```
                    ♠ A K 8 7 4
                    ♡ A K
                    ◊ K 7
                    ♣ 7 6 5 4
    ♠ 10 5                         ♠ Q J 9 3
    ♡ 10 7 4 3                     ♡ Q 8 6 2
    ◊ Q J 10 9                     ◊ 8 4 3
    ♣ Q 9 2                        ♣ 10 8
                    ♠ 6 2
                    ♡ J 9 5
                    ◊ A 6 5 2
                    ♣ A K J 3
```

Contract: 6 ♣
Opening Lead: ◊ Queen

Declarer won the diamond king and took a club finesse. West won and led another diamond. Declarer won and drew trumps. He cashed the A-K of spades and ruffed a spade. West discarded and declarer still lost a spade trick. Down one.

Question: Can you suggest a cure for this declarer's finesse addiction?

Refer him to Frank Stewart. Frank writes a terrific daily newspaper column. He often receives letters from the Society of Finessers complaining finesses never work in his columns. As an example, "Sir: We must protest your disdain for the finesse, an honorable technique that wins half the time---except in your deals."

Frank's not anti-finesse; he is just against those that aren't logical when there is a better line of play. His daily columns provide wonderful tips on declarer play.

At the other table, declarer cashed the A-K of trumps. He then had plenty of time, entries, and trumps to set up the fifth spade, losing just one trump trick.

NO FINESSE: TIMING FOR SECOND SUIT

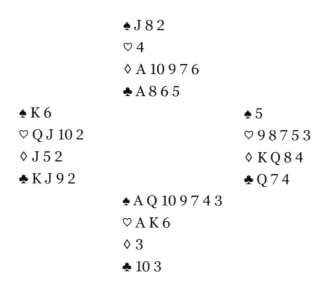

♠ J 8 2
♡ 4
♢ A 10 9 7 6
♣ A 8 6 5

♠ K 6
♡ Q J 10 2
♢ J 5 2
♣ K J 9 2

♠ 5
♡ 9 8 7 5 3
♢ K Q 8 4
♣ Q 7 4

♠ A Q 10 9 7 4 3
♡ A K 6
♢ 3
♣ 10 3

Contract: 6 ♠
Opening Lead: ♡ Queen

Declarer won the opening lead and without much of a plan, ruffed a heart. He took a trump finesse, West won the king, and returned a trump. Declarer lost a club at the end. Down one. With a club lead, it would have been over sooner.

Question: Could you have taken advantage of not receiving a club lead?

At the other table, declarer received the same lead, but formed a plan. Try to set up the diamonds and that required entries. He led the spade ace, both opponents following low. He played a diamond to the ace and ruffed a diamond. Now a heart ruff and another diamond ruff, both followed.

There was still a high diamond out. Needing an entry, declarer ruffed his good high heart. One more diamond ruff established the last diamond.

He gave the opponents their high trump. The club ace was the entry to the good diamond, to discard the club.

63

NO FINESSE: A SECOND SUIT, WHICH ONE

♠ J 10 3
♡ J 10 4
◊ K J 8 5 2
♣ A K

♠ Q 9 4 2   ♠ A 8 7 6
♡ K 6   ♡ 7 3
◊ 6 4   ◊ Q 10 9
♣ Q J 10 5 3   ♣ 9 8 6 2

♠ K 5
♡ A Q 9 8 5 2
◊ A 7 3
♣ 7 4

Contract: 4 ♡

Opening Lead: ♣ Queen

Declarer won the opening lead and lost a trump finesse. He won the club return, drew trumps and cashed the ace of diamonds. He led a diamond to the jack, East won the queen and returned a low spade. Declarer had to guess. Down one.

When comparing with his teammates, declarer asked, "How did he guess the spades?" "He didn't," replied his teammate.

Question: How would you guess the spades?

Trick question. At the other table, declarer took no finesses. After winning the second club, he started the spades. Even if he misguessed, he had time to set up the spade ten to discard the diamond loser.

He could have led the king of spades from his hand. He would lose only two spades and one heart, taking no finesses at the end.

FINESSE? WHAT'S THE HURRY? OTHER CHANCES

```
                    ♠ 7 5
                    ♡ Q J 8 6 2
                    ◊ K 8 6 4 2
                    ♣ 6
    ♠ K 9 4                         ♠ 10 8 6 3 2
    ♡ 7 4                           ♡ 5
    ◊ A 9 5 3                       ◊ Q J 10
    ♣ Q 9 8 3                       ♣ K 10 5 2
                    ♠ A Q J
                    ♡ A K 10 9 3
                    ◊ 7
                    ♣ A J 7 4
```

Contract: 6 ♡

Opening Lead: ♡ 4

Declarer won the opening lead and drew the last trump. With myopic vision, he took a spade finesse. Down one. At least it was quick.

Question: There must be a better line than the play which if wrong, boom.

If more than one line is available, if possible, try one that if wrong, at least you are not down immediately. What kind of hand is this? Unclear. Declarer played A-K of trumps and led a diamond.

West won the ace and led a club. Declarer won, ruffed a club, and with ruffs, was able to set up the diamonds as a second suit to discard the spade losers.

If East had the diamond ace or the suit broke badly, the spade finesse was always there as a LAST RESORT.

NO FINESSES PLEASE

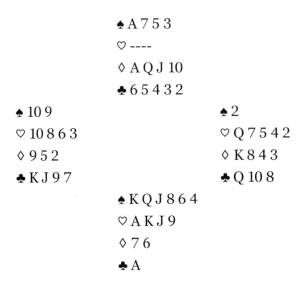

♠ A 7 5 3
♥ ----
♦ A Q J 10
♣ 6 5 4 3 2

♠ 10 9
♥ 10 8 6 3
♦ 9 5 2
♣ K J 9 7

♠ 2
♥ Q 7 5 4 2
♦ K 8 4 3
♣ Q 10 8

♠ K Q J 8 6 4
♥ A K J 9
♦ 7 6
♣ A

Contract: 7 ♠

Opening Lead: ♠ 10

Declarer won the opening lead and drew the last trump. He cashed the A-K of hearts discarding two diamonds and ruffed a heart. When the heart queen did not fall, he finally took a diamond finesse. Down one. Not a strong effort.

Question: Would you have found a stronger line of play?

Nothing was 100% but there was an 85% line. The other declarer won the same opening lead (nice play) and cashed the club ace. He crossed to the spade ace and ruffed a club. He cashed the A-K of hearts and ruffed a heart. He ruffed another club, ruffed a heart and ruffed one more club.

The last club was now good to discard the losing diamond. If clubs had not divided 4-3, declarer had the diamond finesse as a LAST RESORT.

♣ 6-5-4-3-2 may not look like much, but a second suit is a second suit. You just have to look for it.

NO FINESSE: A SECOND SUIT

        ♠ K 8
        ♡ A 10 6 3 2
        ◊ K 8 6 3 2
        ♣ K

♠ 2   ♠ Q 7 3
♡ 7 4   ♡ K 8 5
◊ J 9 7 4   ◊ Q 10 5
♣ Q J 9 5 4 2   ♣ 10 8 6 3

        ♠ A J 10 9 6 5 4
        ♡ Q J 9
        ◊ A
        ♣ A 7

Contract: 6 ♠
Opening Lead: ♣ Queen

Declarer won the opening lead and cashed the A-K of trumps. Unlucky to have a trump loser, he tried a heart finesse. Down one. Sad, nice hand.

Question: Was there a different line of play than the 50% heart finesse?

At the other table, declarer wanted to avoid the finesse if possible. What about a second suit, all those diamonds? He won the opening lead and cashed the diamond ace.

Next came a trump to the king and a diamond ruff. Short on entries, he ruffed the club ace, the key play, and ruffed another diamond. Now he played the spade ace and conceded a spade.

The heart ace was the entry to the diamonds, to discard the losing hearts.

NO FINESSE: TRY FOR THE SECOND SUIT

```
                        ♠ A Q
                        ♡ J 7 4 3 2
                        ◊ A K J 10
                        ♣ 6 5
        ♠ 8 7 2                         ♠ 5 4
        ♡ K 10 8 6                      ♡ A Q 9
        ◊ 8 7                           ◊ 9 6 3
        ♣ K 10 3 2                      ♣ J 9 8 7 4
                        ♠ K J 10 9 6 3
                        ♡ 5
                        ◊ Q 5 4 2
                        ♣ A Q
```

Contract: 6 ♠

Opening Lead: ♠ 2

Declarer, Mr. Finesse, won the opening lead and drew trumps. He couldn't wait to take a club finesse, down one. He would do well in a Speedball event.

Question: Do you see a better line of play?

Perhaps. The finesse can wait. The chance of a 4-3 heart break exceeds the 50% chance of the club finesse.

Using the diamonds as entries, the other declarer set up the heart suit. He discarded his club loser on the last good heart.

FINESSE OR SECOND SUIT?

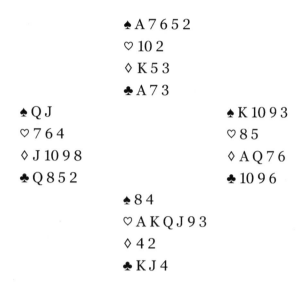

```
              ♠ A 7 6 5 2
              ♡ 10 2
              ◇ K 5 3
              ♣ A 7 3
♠ Q J                           ♠ K 10 9 3
♡ 7 6 4                         ♡ 8 5
◇ J 10 9 8                      ◇ A Q 7 6
♣ Q 8 5 2                       ♣ 10 9 6
              ♠ 8 4
              ♡ A K Q J 9 3
              ◇ 4 2
              ♣ K J 4
```

Contract: 4 ♡
Opening Lead: ◇ Jack

Declarer ducked the opening lead. West continued with the ten and a third diamond (not best). Declarer ruffed and drew trumps. He then played a club to his jack, losing to West, and lost a spade later for down one.

Question: Was this the best plan? How would you have played four hearts?

How about trying to set up the spades in dummy? The other declarer, rather than taking a 50% finesse, knew that if spades were no worse than 4-2, an 84% chance, he would not need the club finesse.

At trick four, he played a low spade from both hands, preserving an entry. Then using the trump ten and the two black aces in dummy, it was easy to set up the fifth spade to discard his club loser.

Note that better defense by East is to overtake the diamond at trick two, and switch to the club ten, attacking the entry in dummy before declarer can start the spades.

ONE FINESSE 50%, TWO 75%, NONE 100%

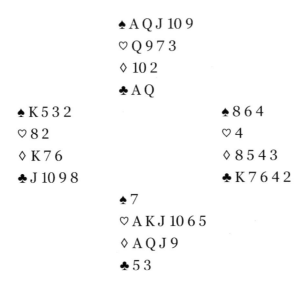

♠ A Q J 10 9
♡ Q 9 7 3
◊ 10 2
♣ A Q

♠ K 5 3 2
♡ 8 2
◊ K 7 6
♣ J 10 9 8

♠ 8 6 4
♡ 4
◊ 8 5 4 3
♣ K 7 6 4 2

♠ 7
♡ A K J 10 6 5
◊ A Q J 9
♣ 5 3

Contract: 6 ♡
Opening Lead: ♣ Jack

Declarer considered his options and saw lots of finesses. He could win the club ace and take a spade finesse to throw his club loser, a 50% play. If he finessed first in clubs, then in diamonds, he had a 75% chance. He took the 75% option.

Unfortunately, both minor kings were offside. Down one.

Question: Unlucky or was there a better line of play?

The other declarer took door number three, the 100% line. He won the opening lead, drew trumps, cashed the spade ace, and led the spade queen, discarding his last club when East didn't cover.

The remaining good spades took care of the three diamond losers.

LOSER-
ON-
LOSER

SPOT CARDS MEAN A LOT, LOSER-ON-LOSER

```
                     ♠ 9 7 4 2
                     ♡ 8 6 5 3
                     ◊ 8 6 2
                     ♣ A Q
        ♠ K Q J 5 3                    ♠ 8 6
        ♡ 9                            ♡ J 7 4
        ◊ K J 10 5                     ◊ 9 4 3
        ♣ J 10 2                       ♣ K 9 7 6 5
                     ♠ A 10
                     ♡ A K Q 10 2
                     ◊ A Q 7
                     ♣ 8 4 3
```

South	West	North	East
1 ♡	1 ♠	2 ♡	P
4 ♡		All Pass	

Opening Lead: ♠ King

Declarer won the opening lead and drew trumps. And, of course, started finessing. The club finesse lost, the diamond finesse lost, he lost one spade, one club, and two diamonds. "Sorry, partner," moaned South. "Very unlucky."

Question: What do you think North is thinking about South's "luck?"

At the other table, the declarer asked himself, how can I make this hand should both finesses be offside? Trick one went king, two, eight, ace. He drew trumps and led the spade ten. West won the spade queen and continued with the club jack.

Declarer played the ace and led the spade nine, discarding a diamond. West won, but now the spade seven was high to take care of the other diamond loser. The defense cashed a club. Declarer lost two spades and one club, making four hearts. Who needs luck? Who needs finesses?

NO FINESSES: LOSER – ON - LOSER PLAY

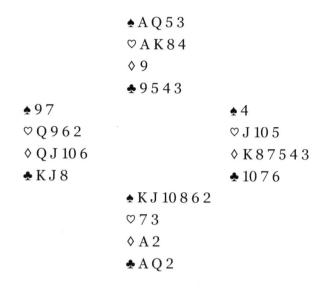

```
                ♠ A Q 5 3
                ♡ A K 8 4
                ◊ 9
                ♣ 9 5 4 3
  ♠ 9 7                        ♠ 4
  ♡ Q 9 6 2                    ♡ J 10 5
  ◊ Q J 10 6                   ◊ K 8 7 5 4 3
  ♣ K J 8                      ♣ 10 7 6
                ♠ K J 10 8 6 2
                ♡ 7 3
                ◊ A 2
                ♣ A Q 2
```

Contract: 6 ♠

Opening Lead: ◊ Queen

Declarer won the opening lead. He stared at dummy's club nine, wishing it were in his hand rather than the dummy. Then it would be an easy endplay.

After drawing trumps, he took an unimaginative line of play, a club finesse. Down one.

Question: Sorry, no club nine, but can't you still come up with a better plan?

The other declarer wasn't going down so fast. After drawing trumps, she played the A-K of hearts and ruffed a heart. Now she ruffed her remaining diamond and led the last heart. When East showed out, what did declarer do?

No, she did not ruff the heart. She claimed! She discarded a club. West was endplayed. A club return into her A-Q or a ruff/sluff. Making six spades.

NO FINESSES: LOSER – ON - LOSER

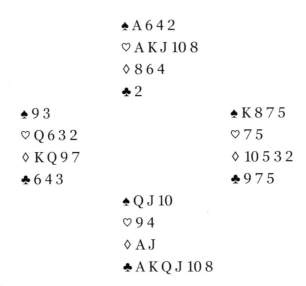

                    ♠ A 6 4 2
                    ♡ A K J 10 8
                    ◊ 8 6 4
                    ♣ 2
    ♠ 9 3   ♠ K 8 7 5
    ♡ Q 6 3 2   ♡ 7 5
    ◊ K Q 9 7   ◊ 10 5 3 2
    ♣ 6 4 3   ♣ 9 7 5
                    ♠ Q J 10
                    ♡ 9 4
                    ◊ A J
                    ♣ A K Q J 10 8

Contract: 6 ♣

Opening Lead: ◊ King

Too many choices. What to do with the diamond loser? Take a spade finesse? Or a heart finesse? Or try to ruff out the heart queen? Not a lot of dummy entries.

Declarer won the opening lead and cashed the A-K of hearts. When the queen failed to drop, he drew trumps and took a spade finesse. Maybe he should have read my book. "Minus 50?" asked North.

Question: Was there some way to avoid these finesses?

The other declarer had bought this book. She won the opening lead and drew trumps. She played the A-K of hearts, and continued a heart, discarding her losing diamond.

"Plus 920?" asked North.

74

NO FINESSE, LOSER – ON - LOSER

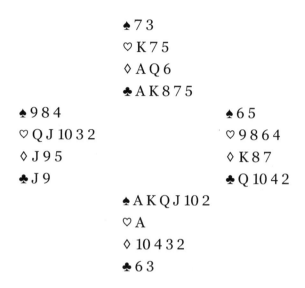

♠ 7 3
♥ K 7 5
♦ A Q 6
♣ A K 8 7 5

♠ 9 8 4
♥ Q J 10 3 2
♦ J 9 5
♣ J 9

♠ 6 5
♥ 9 8 6 4
♦ K 8 7
♣ Q 10 4 2

♠ A K Q J 10 2
♥ A
♦ 10 4 3 2
♣ 6 3

Contract: 6 ♠

Opening Lead: ♥ Queen

Declarer won the opening lead. Hoping to set up the clubs, he drew trumps and cashed the A-K of clubs and ruffed a club. But clubs were 4-2, and with too few entries, tried a diamond finesse.

He ended losing two diamond tricks, down one.

Question: Another unlucky hand, or was there a better line of play?

The other declarer, always looking to avoid a finesse, discarded a diamond when East followed to the third club. If West followed, clubs were 3-3, fine.

If West showed out, East was endplayed. A heart return would give declarer the extra entry he needed. With a diamond return, the hand was over.

NO FINESSES: REMEMBER THE BIDDING

```
                    ♠ Q J 8 3
                    ♡ 8 6 4
                    ◇ A 10 3
                    ♣ A 9 3
        ♠ 9 2                       ♠ 6 5
        ♡ K Q J 9 5                 ♡ 10
        ◇ K 7 4                     ◇ J 9 8 6
        ♣ K 10 5                    ♣ Q 8 7 6 4 2
                    ♠ A K 10 7 4
                    ♡ A 7 3 2
                    ◇ Q 5 2
                    ♣ J
```

West	North	East	South
1 ♡	P	P	1 ♠
P	2 ♡	P	3 ♠
P	4 ♠	All Pass	

Opening Lead: ♡ King

Declarer won the opening lead and drew trumps. He led a club to the ace and a diamond to his queen. West took the king, cashed two hearts, and played a club. Declarer ruffed.

When declarer tried a diamond to dummy's ten, he was down one.

Question: Was this unlucky, two finesses losing, a 75% chance?

At the other table, declarer remembered the bidding. And saw lots of trumps in both hands. No finesses, thank you. She took the club ace at trick two, ruffed a club, drew trumps and ruffed dummy's last club.

The stage was set. Now she played a heart. West took two heart tricks. When West led a fourth heart, declarer discarded a diamond from dummy instead of ruffing, a loser – on – loser.

West was stuck; he had to lead away from his diamond king or concede a ruff/sluff. Making four spades, losing three heart tricks.

NO FINESSE: LOSER – ON – LOSER ENDPLAY

```
                    ♠ 8 6
                    ♡ A Q 4
                    ◊ A J 10 2
                    ♣ 10 9 3 2
   ♠ Q J 10 5 3                      ♠ 9 7 4 2
   ♡ J 9 8                           ♡ K 10 7 6
   ◊ 4                               ◊ 8 3
   ♣ Q 8 6 5                         ♣ J 7 4
                    ♠ A K
                    ♡ 5 3 2
                    ◊ K Q 9 7 6 5
                    ♣ A K
```

Contract: 6 ◊
Opening Lead: ♠ Queen

Declarer won the opening lead and drew trumps. He took a heart finesse. East won and returned a spade. Declarer had another heart loser at the end. Down one.

Question: Do you recognize what type of hand this is?

Lots of trumps in both hands, so think elimination and/or endplay. Try to avoid finesses.

At the other table, declarer won the opening spade lead, cashed the other high spade, cashed the A-K of clubs, and drew trumps with the A-J.

He led the club ten. When the jack appeared, he discarded a heart. East didn't have the club queen to exit, and West could not afford to overtake. Unless he had another club, East was endplayed, a heart into the A-Q or a ruff/sluff.

NO FINESSE: LOSER – ON – LOSER ENDPLAY

```
                        ♠ K J 4
                        ♡ K 7 6 4
                        ◊ 10 7 2
                        ♣ 9 6 5
        ♠ 10 8 7 6 5 2              ♠ Q 9
        ♡ 10                        ♡ 8 5
        ◊ A K J                     ◊ Q 9 6 5 3
        ♣ K J 2                     ♣ 10 8 7 4
                        ♠ A 3
                        ♡ A Q J 9 3 2
                        ◊ 8 4
                        ♣ A Q 3
```

South	West	North	East
1 ♡	1 ♠	2 ♡	P
4 ♡		All Pass	

Opening Lead: ◊ Ace

Declarer ruffed the third round of diamonds and drew trumps. He played the spade ace and a spade to the jack, planning on discarding a club loser.

Whoops. He still had one club loser at the end. Down one.

Question: Unlucky? After all, West did overcall in spades.

At the other table, after the same start, the declarer drew trumps, then cashed the A-K of spades. His good plan was to lead the spade jack, discard a club and endplay West.

Hello, the spade queen fell.

78

FINESSE? LOSER – ON – LOSER RUFFING FINESSE

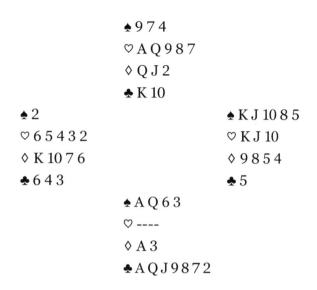

                ♠ 9 7 4
                ♡ A Q 9 8 7
                ◇ Q J 2
                ♣ K 10
♠ 2   ♠ K J 10 8 5
♡ 6 5 4 3 2   ♡ K J 10
◇ K 10 7 6   ◇ 9 8 5 4
♣ 6 4 3   ♣ 5
                ♠ A Q 6 3
                ♡ - - - -
                ◇ A 3
                ♣ A Q J 9 8 7 2

Contract: 6 ♣ (East bid spades)
Opening Lead: ♠ 2

Declarer won the opening lead and led a trump to dummy. He took a diamond finesse. West won and returned a trump. South still had to lose a spade at the end. Down one.

Question: Was there a successful line of play?

At the other table, declarer found a better way to use all his assets. He cashed the ace of diamonds at trick two, then went to dummy with a trump. He discarded his last diamond on the heart ace, and led the diamond queen.

If covered, his plan was to ruff, enter dummy with a trump, and discard a spade on the good diamond. If not covered, he would discard a spade, When West won, the remaining high diamond would be good.

Either way, declarer would lose only one trick, a spade or a diamond. Making six clubs.

NO FINESSE: LOSER – ON - LOSER ENDPLAY

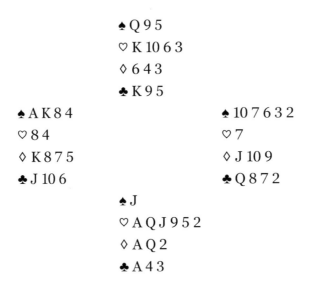

```
                    ♠ Q 9 5
                    ♡ K 10 6 3
                    ◊ 6 4 3
                    ♣ K 9 5
  ♠ A K 8 4                         ♠ 10 7 6 3 2
  ♡ 8 4                             ♡ 7
  ◊ K 8 7 5                         ◊ J 10 9
  ♣ J 10 6                          ♣ Q 8 7 2
                    ♠ J
                    ♡ A Q J 9 5 2
                    ◊ A Q 2
                    ♣ A 4 3
```

Contract: 4 ♡

Opening Lead: ♠ Ace

West led the spade ace and switched to the club jack. Declarer won, drew trumps, and took a diamond finesse. He lost one spade, one club, and two diamonds. Down one.

Question: What type of hand is this? The answer is often the key to success.

Whenever you have lots of trumps in both hands, think elimination and endplays. At the other table, declarer had a different game plan. He ducked the club jack and won the club continuation with the ace. (Should East have overtaken?)

He cashed the A-K of trumps and ruffed a spade. Then he played a club to the king and led the spade queen, discarding a diamond.

West was endplayed. A diamond return into the A-Q, or a spade and a ruff/sluff conceded the contract. Declarer lost two spades and one club.

NO FINESSE: SORT OF LOSER – ON – LOSER

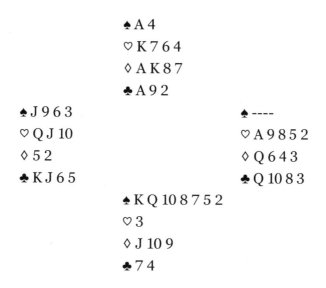

```
                        ♠ A 4
                        ♡ K 7 6 4
                        ◇ A K 8 7
                        ♣ A 9 2
        ♠ J 9 6 3                       ♠ ----
        ♡ Q J 10                        ♡ A 9 8 5 2
        ◇ 5 2                           ◇ Q 6 4 3
        ♣ K J 6 5                       ♣ Q 10 8 3
                        ♠ K Q 10 8 7 5 2
                        ♡ 3
                        ◇ J 10 9
                        ♣ 7 4
```

Contract: 4 ♠

Opening Lead: ♡ Queen

Declarer ruffed the second heart and led a trump to the ace. He returned to his hand with a trump, cashed another high trump, and took a diamond finesse. East won and returned a club.

Declarer tried to discard a club on the diamonds, but West ruffed in and cashed a club. Down one.

Question: What is a better line of play? What type of hand might this be?

The other declarer timed the hand better. After three rounds of trumps, he cashed the A-K of diamonds, no finesse. The queen didn't fall but he was in control. He gave up a diamond, staying a step ahead of the defenders.

The last diamond was high and declarer still had the club ace. He discarded his club loser on the last diamond as West ruffed in. He lost one spade, one heart, and one diamond. He did not lose control.

AVOIDING A FINESSE: LOSER – ON LOSER

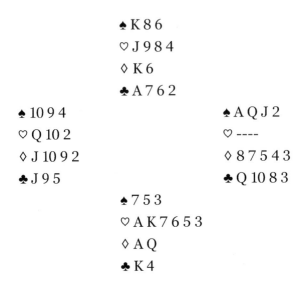

```
                    ♠ K 8 6
                    ♡ J 9 8 4
                    ◊ K 6
                    ♣ A 7 6 2
      ♠ 10 9 4                      ♠ A Q J 2
      ♡ Q 10 2                      ♡ ----
      ◊ J 10 9 2                    ◊ 8 7 5 4 3
      ♣ J 9 5                       ♣ Q 10 8 3
                    ♠ 7 5 3
                    ♡ A K 7 6 5 3
                    ◊ A Q
                    ♣ K 4
```

Contract: 4 ♡

Opening Lead: ◊ Jack

East had been wishing for a spade lead, but West led a diamond. Declarer won the king and led the heart jack in case East had ♡ Q 10 2 and covered.

He cashed the A-K of trumps and led towards the spade king. Down one.

Question: The winning line of play requires a little foresight. Do you see it?

What would you like? You would like East to play a spade. Can you arrange that? Perhaps. The other declarer won the first trick in hand, saving a dummy entry.

He cashed the A-K of trumps. He cashed the A-K of clubs and ruffed a club. Now he returned to dummy with the diamond king and played his last club. When East followed, declarer discarded a spade.

Wish come true! East had to play a spade or concede a ruff/sluff. Either way, ten tricks.

NO FINESSE: LOSER – ON – LOSER ENDPLAY

```
                    ♠ 8 7 2
                    ♡ 8 7 5 2
                    ♢ 3
                    ♣ A J 10 7 2
        ♠ A Q 6                      ♠ J 10 9 4
        ♡ Q J 10 9 3                 ♡ K 6 4
        ♢ Q J 7 4                    ♢ K 9 6 5 2
        ♣ Q                          ♣ 9
                    ♠ K 5 3
                    ♡ A
                    ♢ A 10 8
                    ♣ K 8 6 5 4 3
```

South	West	North	East
1 ♣	1 ♡	2 ♣	2 ♡
5 ♣		All Pass	

Opening Lead: ♡ Queen

Declarer won the opening lead and drew trumps. With little effort, he went to dummy and led towards his spade king. He lost three spade tricks. Down one.

Question: Is there a way to avoid this finesse? (Of course)

At the other table, declarer was in no rush, and remembered the bidding. After drawing the trumps, he played the diamond ace and ruffed a diamond.

He ruffed a heart and ruffed another diamond. Then another heart ruff, leaving one heart in dummy.

He returned to dummy with a trump. Now he led the last heart and discarded a spade. West was endplayed. The best he could do was cash the spade ace. Making five clubs.

WHICH FINESSE? NO FINESSES

♠ A J
♡ 9 6 4 2
◊ 4 3 2
♣ A 9 8 4

♠ 10 7 6   ♠ Q 9 4 3 2
♡ K Q 10 8 5   ♡ J 7 3
◊ K J 9 6   ◊ 10 8 7
♣ 6   ♣ 7 5

♠ K 8 5
♡ A
◊ A Q 5
♣ K Q J 10 3 2

South	West	North	East
1 ♣	1 ♡	2 ♣	P
2 ♡	P	2 ♠	P
6 ♣	All Pass		

Opening Lead: ♡ King

Declarer won the opening lead and drew trumps. He took a spade finesse, hoping to discard a diamond. East won and returned a heart. Declarer ruffed the heart and took a diamond finesse. Down one.

"I guess if there had been a third finesse, you would have taken that too," said North. "Where were you during the bidding?"

Question: What was North referring to?

At the other table, declarer took no finesses. He won the opening lead, crossed to dummy with a trump and ruffed a heart high. He went back to dummy with a trump and ruffed another heart high, eliminating East's hearts.

He played the A-K of spades and ruffed a spade. He led dummy's last heart and discarded a diamond, a loser-on-loser. West was endplayed. His choices were a diamond return into the A-Q or a ruff/sluff. Making six clubs.

84

NO FINESSE: LOSER – ON - LOSER ENDPLAY

```
                    ♠ Q 10 9 7 6
                    ♡ Q 6
                    ◇ 9 5 3
                    ♣ A Q 6
        ♠ 4                         ♠ 3
        ♡ A K J 10 7 3             ♡ 8 5 4 2
        ◇ K J 8                    ◇ 7 6 4
        ♣ J 10 9                   ♣ K 8 7 4 3
                    ♠ A K J 8 5 2
                    ♡ 9
                    ◇ A Q 10 2
                    ♣ 5 2
```

South	West	North	East
1 ♠	2 ♡	3 ♡	P
4 ♠		All Pass	

Opening Lead: ♡ Ace

West led the heart ace and switched to the club jack. Declarer lost a club finesse and East returned a diamond. Declarer tried the ten, West won the jack. Declarer ruffed the heart return. There was still another losing diamond finesse at the end. Down one.

"My usual bad luck," moaned South. "Three finesses lost."

Question: How many finesses did the other declarer take to make four spades?

Only one. Play started the same, but at trick two this declarer won the club ace and played the heart queen. Instead of ruffing, he discarded his last club.

West won and returned a club. Declarer ruffed, played a trump to dummy drawing the trumps, and ruffed dummy's club.

He went to dummy with a trump and led a diamond. It didn't matter if he played the ten or queen. West was in and endplayed. Making four spades.

FINESSE? NO, OTHER OPTIONS

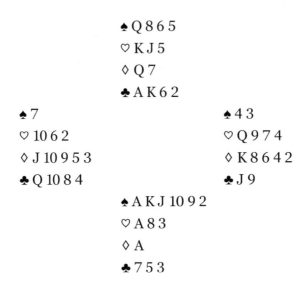

```
                    ♠ Q 8 6 5
                    ♡ K J 5
                    ◊ Q 7
                    ♣ A K 6 2
    ♠ 7                              ♠ 4 3
    ♡ 10 6 2                         ♡ Q 9 7 4
    ◊ J 10 9 5 3                     ◊ K 8 6 4 2
    ♣ Q 10 8 4                       ♣ J 9
                    ♠ A K J 10 9 2
                    ♡ A 8 3
                    ◊ A
                    ♣ 7 5 3
```

Contract: 6 ♠

Opening Lead: ◊ Jack

Declarer won the opening lead and drew trumps. Wanting to avoid the heart finesse, he first tried the clubs, hoping for a 3-3 split.

When that failed, he tried the heart finesse. Down one.

Question: Do you see any other chances or was declarer just unlucky?

At the other table, declarer drew trumps and cashed the A-K of clubs. However, judging from the opening lead, he played the queen of diamonds. When East covered, declarer discarded his last club.

If clubs were 3-3 and East had a club to return, declarer could use dummy's last club for a heart discard. Since East didn't have a club to return, the heart or diamond return gave declarer his tenth trick. If East had four clubs, the heart finesse was still a LAST RESORT.

ENDPLAYS, ELIMINATION PLAYS

NO FINESSE, ENDPLAY

```
                    ♠ 9 8 3 2
                    ♡ K 10 2
                    ◇ A J 10 9 7
                    ♣ 3
      ♠ K 5 4                        ♠ J 10 6
      ♡ Q J 9 8 7                    ♡ A 6 5 4
      ◇ 2                            ◇ 3
      ♣ K J 6 2                      ♣ 10 9 8 7 5
                    ♠ A Q 7
                    ♡ 3
                    ◇ K Q 8 6 5 4
                    ♣ A Q 4
```

South	West	North	East
1 ◇	1 ♡	Dbl	4 ♡
Dbl	P	5 ◇	All Pass

Opening Lead: ♡ Queen

Declarer ducked the opening lead. West shifted to a trump. The club finesse was a mirage as it would only provide one spade discard. Declarer played the ace of clubs. He then ruffed his remaining clubs and hearts and led a spade.

He lost two spade tricks, and one heart. Down one.

Question: Could you have made better use of the dummy's assets?

The first declarer was on the right tract, but didn't appreciate dummy's hearts. The other declarer won the trump continuation, played the ace of clubs and ruffed a club. Then he led the heart king. East had to cover.

Declarer ruffed, ruffed his last club and exited dummy with the heart ten, endplaying West. If the heart king was not covered, he planned to discard a spade. Again West would have been endplayed.

NO LOSING FINESSES, TRY SOMETHING ELSE

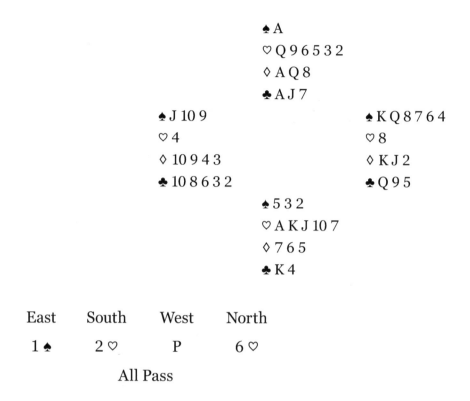

```
                        ♠ A
                        ♡ Q 9 6 5 3 2
                        ◇ A Q 8
                        ♣ A J 7
        ♠ J 10 9                        ♠ K Q 8 7 6 4
        ♡ 4                             ♡ 8
        ◇ 10 9 4 3                      ◇ K J 2
        ♣ 10 8 6 3 2                    ♣ Q 9 5
                        ♠ 5 3 2
                        ♡ A K J 10 7
                        ◇ 7 6 5
                        ♣ K 4
```

East	South	West	North
1 ♠	2 ♡	P	6 ♡
	All Pass		

Opening Lead: ♠ Jack

Declarer won the opening lead and drew trumps. Without much of a game plan, declarer took a club finesse to discard a diamond. East won and returned a spade. Declarer later lost a diamond, down one.

Question: What type of player was this declarer?

Either very inexperienced or in love with finesses. Both finesses were doomed. With twelve HCP's missing, who has them, the opening bidder or the waiter?

The other declarer won the opening lead and came to her hand with a trump. She ruffed a spade and played a club to her king. She ruffed her last spade and played the ace of clubs, then the club jack, discarding a diamond.

East was in. With the spades and clubs eliminated, East was endplayed. A diamond return would be into the A-Q and a spade return would result in a ruff/sluff. Making six hearts. Don't take finesses that can't possibly work.

89

AVOIDING A FINESSE BY COUNTING

```
                        ♠ Q 10 5 4 3
                        ♡ A 7 5 2
                        ◊ 10 3
                        ♣ J 6
         ♠ 8                          ♠ 9 2
         ♡ K J 10 4                   ♡ 9
         ◊ 8 5 4                      ◊ J 9 6 2
         ♣ Q 9 5 3 2                  ♣ A K 10 8 7 4
                        ♠ A K J 7 6
                        ♡ Q 8 6 3
                        ◊ A K Q 7
                        ♣ ----
```

South	West	North	East
1 ♠	P	2 ♠	3 ♣
4 ♣	5 ♣	5 ♡	P
6 ♠	All Pass		

Opening Lead: ♣ 3

Declarer ruffed the opening lead and drew trumps. He ruffed dummy's last club, cashed the high diamonds discarding a heart, and ruffed his last diamond. East followed suit each time. Declarer cashed the heart ace and led a heart. Down one.

Question: Could South have found a winning line?

At the other table, play started the same. But when East followed to the fourth diamond, declarer knew East's shape was 2-0-4-7 or 2-1-4-6. Declarer led a low heart from each hand. Whoever won the trick was endplayed.

If East won, a ruff/sluff was coming. If West won, he had to lead away from the heart king.

THE IMPORTANCE OF THE NINE

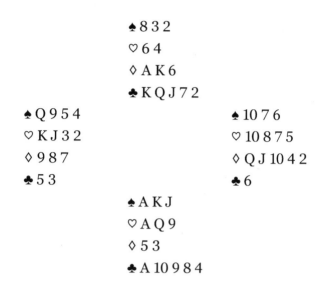

♠ 8 3 2
♡ 6 4
◇ A K 6
♣ K Q J 7 2

♠ Q 9 5 4
♡ K J 3 2
◇ 9 8 7
♣ 5 3

♠ 10 7 6
♡ 10 8 7 5
◇ Q J 10 4 2
♣ 6

♠ A K J
♡ A Q 9
◇ 5 3
♣ A 10 9 8 4

Contract: 6 ♣

Opening Lead: ♣ 3

Declarer drew trumps and started taking finesses. He first took a spade finesse. West won the queen and returned a diamond. Declarer tried a heart to the queen. Down one.

Question: What is the biggest card in the South hand?

The nine of hearts makes six clubs cold. This is a basic elimination play. Draw trumps, eliminate the diamonds, and lead towards the ♡ A Q 9, planning on just covering whatever card East plays.

If East plays small, insert the nine. If the nine loses to the ten, West is endplayed. If East plays the ten, insert the queen. Same story.

On this hand, West is endplayed, having to return a heart or a spade.

The importance of the nine cannot be overstated. The A Q 8 doesn't do the same, unless of course you have the nine in the dummy.

NO FINESSE: ENDPLAY (DEFENDER TRIES TO AVOID)

```
                        ♠ J 7 3
                        ♡ A 4 2
                        ◇ 7 5 3 2
                        ♣ 5 4 3
        ♠ 10 4                          ♠ 6 2
        ♡ Q J 10 6                      ♡ K 9 7 5 3
        ◇ Q 10 9                        ◇ J 4
        ♣ K J 10 8                      ♣ 9 7 6 2
                        ♠ A K Q 9 8 5
                        ♡ 8
                        ◇ A K 8 6
                        ♣ A Q
```

Contract: 6 ♠

Opening Lead: ♡ Queen

Declarer won the opening lead and drew trumps. She tried a club finesse. West won the king and led another heart. At least diamonds were 3-2. Down only one.

Question: Unavoidable or was there a better plan?

The declarer at the other table tried something different. He won the opening heart lead and ruffed a heart high. He led a trump to the jack and then ruffed another heart high.

After drawing the last trumps, when they divided 2-2, he cashed the A-K of diamonds and played a third diamond.

West tried to avoid the endplay by discarding the queen, then the ten of diamonds, but was forced to win the third diamond with the nine and lead a club from his king.

TAKING NO FINESSES

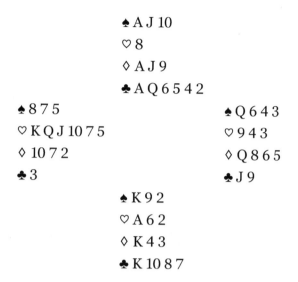

```
              ♠ A J 10
              ♡ 8
              ◇ A J 9
              ♣ A Q 6 5 4 2
♠ 8 7 5                          ♠ Q 6 4 3
♡ K Q J 10 7 5                   ♡ 9 4 3
◇ 10 7 2                         ◇ Q 8 6 5
♣ 3                              ♣ J 9
              ♠ K 9 2
              ♡ A 6 2
              ◇ K 4 3
              ♣ K 10 8 7
```

Contract: 6 ♣ (West preempts in hearts)
Opening Lead: ♡ King

Declarer won the opening lead and drew trumps. He had a two-way finesse in spades and one-way finesse in diamonds. After losing the diamond finesse, he said, "Guess I'll play for 'split queens,' partner," and lost a spade trick to East.

Down one. Split queens, really?

Question: How would you have handled these finesses?

At the other table, declarer was ready to claim after the opening lead. "I'm taking no finesses," he said. "I'm going to draw trumps, ruff my two hearts, and cash the A-K of diamonds. If the queen of diamonds has not fallen, I'll play a diamond and one of you will have to break the spade suit."

East/West folded their cards.

WHICH FINESSE? NO FINESSE

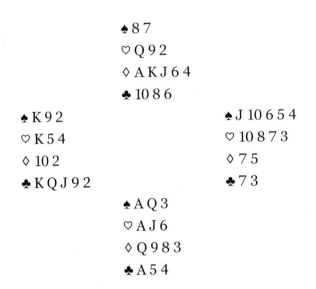

$\spadesuit$ 8 7
$\heartsuit$ Q 9 2
$\diamond$ A K J 6 4
$\clubsuit$ 10 8 6

$\spadesuit$ K 9 2 $\spadesuit$ J 10 6 5 4
$\heartsuit$ K 5 4 $\heartsuit$ 10 8 7 3
$\diamond$ 10 2 $\diamond$ 7 5
$\clubsuit$ K Q J 9 2 $\clubsuit$ 7 3

$\spadesuit$ A Q 3
$\heartsuit$ A J 6
$\diamond$ Q 9 8 3
$\clubsuit$ A 5 4

Contract: 3 NT
Opening Lead: $\clubsuit$ King

Declarer counted eight winners on top. A successful finesse in either major suit would bring this home. He ducked the first two clubs and won the third. Too bad one finesse wasn't into East, the safe hand. West had both kings. Down one.

Question: How did the other declarer make 3 NT? What type of hand is this?

At the other table, declarer saw East follow to the second club. That meant West had five clubs, not six. There was no reason to duck trick two.

After cashing enough diamonds to see West show out, declarer played his remaining club.

When West finished taking three club tricks, he had to play a major, assuring declarer of a ninth trick. Remember, try to put the opponents to work for you.

NO FINESSES PLEASE: ENDPLAY

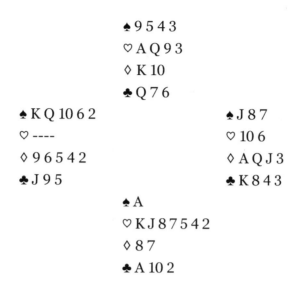

```
              ♠ 9 5 4 3
              ♡ A Q 9 3
              ◇ K 10
              ♣ Q 7 6
♠ K Q 10 6 2                    ♠ J 8 7
♡ ----                         ♡ 10 6
◇ 9 6 5 4 2                     ◇ A Q J 3
♣ J 9 5                        ♣ K 8 4 3
              ♠ A
              ♡ K J 8 7 5 4 2
              ◇ 8 7
              ♣ A 10 2
```

Contract: 4 ♡

Opening Lead: ♠ King

Declarer won the opening lead and drew trumps. He played a club to the queen. East won and returned a spade. Declarer ruffed and led a diamond. East won two diamond tricks.

Declarer took another club finesse, low to his ♣A 10, West won the jack. Zero for three, unlucky as usual. Down one.

Question: How did the other declarer make four hearts?

He won the opening lead and led a heart to dummy's ace. He ruffed a spade. Then a heart to dummy's queen and another spade ruff. Then he played a heart to dummy's nine and ruffed the last spade.

Now with a trump still in each hand, he led a diamond to dummy's king. East could take two diamond tricks, but no matter how the club honors were divided, declarer would lose only one club trick. Making four hearts.

If West had won the second diamond and led a club, declarer would have played low from dummy.

AVOIDING FINESSES WITH "IFFY" SUITS

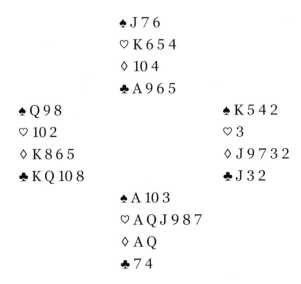

```
                    ♠ J 7 6
                    ♡ K 6 5 4
                    ◇ 10 4
                    ♣ A 9 6 5
    ♠ Q 9 8                        ♠ K 5 4 2
    ♡ 10 2                         ♡ 3
    ◇ K 8 6 5                      ◇ J 9 7 3 2
    ♣ K Q 10 8                     ♣ J 3 2
                    ♠ A 10 3
                    ♡ A Q J 9 8 7
                    ◇ A Q
                    ♣ 7 4
```

Contract: 4 ♡

Opening Lead: ♣ King

Declarer won the opening lead and drew trumps. He took a diamond finesse. West won, cashed the club queen and played a club. Declarer ruffed and had to play the "iffy" spade suit himself for one loser. Down one.

Question: Was there a way to not have to play the "iffy" suit yourself?

Those are the kind of suits you never want to be the one to lead first. At the other table, declarer ducked the opening club lead. West shifted to a trump. Declarer drew the last trump, and led a club to the ace. He ruffed a club and led to dummy's heart king.

He ruffed dummy's last club. Then he cashed the diamond ace and exited the diamond queen (another 'mirage' queen, it could have been a deuce).
Whoever won had to start the spades. Declarer lost one spade, one diamond, and one club. Making four hearts.

THREE SUITS TO FINESSE?

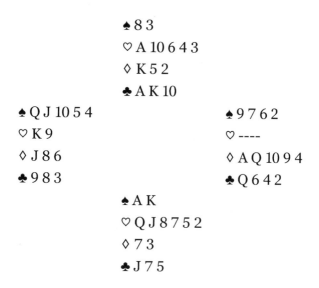

♠ 8 3
♡ A 10 6 4 3
◇ K 5 2
♣ A K 10

♠ Q J 10 5 4
♡ K 9
◇ J 8 6
♣ 9 8 3

♠ 9 7 6 2
♡ ----
◇ A Q 10 9 4
♣ Q 6 4 2

♠ A K
♡ Q J 8 7 5 2
◇ 7 3
♣ J 7 5

Contract: 4 ♡

Opening Lead: ♠ Queen

Declarer won the opening lead and led the heart queen. West played the nine smoothly. With eleven trumps, declarer played the ace. East showed out.

Declarer played a spade back to his hand and took a club finesse. East won and returned a club. Declarer later lost two diamond tricks, down one.

Question: Unlucky, or would you have had a better game plan?

There were three possible finesses. The first declarer rejected the finesse he should have taken, and took two finesses that could have been avoided. He went zero for three. It's a bridge hand, not a heart suit.

The other declarer also counted eleven trumps. After winning the opening lead, he cashed the other high spade and took a heart finesse. If it lost, East would be endplayed. If it won, he could afford three minor suit losers. He went one for one. Making four hearts.

ASSUMPTIONS, NO FINESSES

```
                    ♠ 10 3 2
                    ♡ 8
                    ◊ A Q 7 6 4 2
                    ♣ A J 9
        ♠ A K                         ♠ 9 5
        ♡ K J 6 5 4 3                 ♡ 9 7 2
        ◊ 8 3                         ◊ K J 10 5
        ♣ 10 8 4                      ♣ Q 7 6 2
                    ♠ Q J 8 7 6 4
                    ♡ A Q 10
                    ◊ 9
                    ♣ K 5 3
```

South	West	North	East
1 ♠	2 ♡	3 ◊	3 ♡
3 ♠	P	4 ♠	All Pass

Opening Lead: ♠ Ace

West played the A-K of spades, then the diamond eight. With a probable late heart loser, and not enough dummy entries to set up the diamonds, declarer played a club to the jack. He lost a heart at the end. Down one.

Question: How would you have played? Can you avoid the losing club finesse?

Maybe double dummy, an intra-finesse; lead the jack, covered, then finesse the ten. But the other declarer assumed West had the king of hearts and could be endplayed. After the A-K of spades and diamond shift, he won the ace of diamonds and ruffed a diamond.

He led the heart queen. West had only hearts and clubs and was endplayed. West exited a small club and the nine forced East's queen. If West had another diamond to exit, then the diamonds would have been 3-3.

FINESSE BUT LET THE OPPONENTS GO FIRST

```
                    ♠ A 7 2
                    ♡ Q J 9 8 2
                    ◊ A 9
                    ♣ K J 7
       ♠ K J 10 5 4              ♠ Q 9
       ♡ 6                       ♡ 4 3
       ◊ K Q 10 6                ◊ 7 5 4 3 2
       ♣ x x 2                   ♣ x x 4 3
                    ♠ 8 6 3
                    ♡ A K 10 7 5
                    ◊ J 8
                    ♣ A 9 6
```

Contract: 4 ♡

Opening Lead: ◊ King

Declarer had two spades and a diamond to lose, no possible discards anywhere. He won the opening lead, drew trumps, and took a club finesse.

Question: Could you have improved the odds from 50%? How about to 75%?

The other declarer drew trumps and played back a diamond. West won and shifted to spades. Declarer won and returned a spade. The defenders took two spade tricks. It was time to play clubs, but the opponents had to go first.

If it's East, it's into the K-J, so assume West is on lead.
There are four possible club layouts of the significant cards:

West	East	
Q 10 x opposite	x x x	You make no matter what you play
Q x x	10 x x	Play low, win and finesse West
10 x x	Q x x	Play low, East has to play the queen
x x x	Q 10 x	You lose, down one

In three out of four cases, you win, 75%. Better "after you," than you first.

NO FINESSES, YOU GO FIRST, THANK YOU

```
                    ♠ K 8 7
                    ♡ A K Q 10
                    ◇ K 6 4
                    ♣ 7 6 5
        ♠ Q 10 9                      ♠ A 5 3 2
        ♡ 5 3                         ♡ 7 6
        ◇ Q 10 8 5                    ◇ 9 7 2
        ♣ 10 9 8 4                    ♣ K J 3 2
                    ♠ J 6 4
                    ♡ J 9 8 4 2
                    ◇ A J 3
                    ♣ A Q
```

Contract: 4 ♡

Opening Lead: ♣ 10

The opening lead gave declarer a trick he would have won anyhow, but he could still lose a diamond and three spades, an "iffy" suit. After drawing trumps, he started finessing, first losing the diamond finesse, and then playing the spades.

He managed to make his dream come true. Down one.

Question: Was this just a "Declarer Nightmare" or could you have handled it?

The other declarer, after the same opening lead, thought "I have opponents, I'll let them do the work." After drawing trumps, declarer cashed the club ace, went to the diamond king and ruffed a club.

Now he cashed the diamond ace and played the diamond jack. No finesse, thank you. The defenders had to break the "iffy" spade suit.

Declarer could not lose three spade tricks, regardless of the layout.

TWO FINESSES? ONE IS PLENTY, I HAVE THE KEY CARD

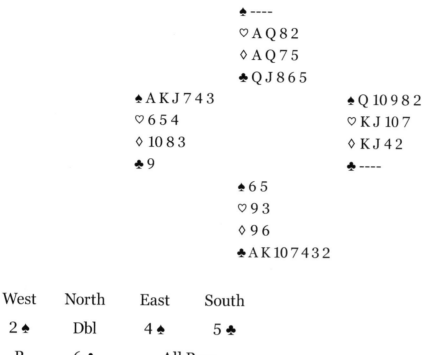

```
                    ♠ ----
                    ♡ A Q 8 2
                    ◇ A Q 7 5
                    ♣ Q J 8 6 5
    ♠ A K J 7 4 3                 ♠ Q 10 9 8 2
    ♡ 6 5 4                       ♡ K J 10 7
    ◇ 10 8 3                      ◇ K J 4 2
    ♣ 9                           ♣ ----
                    ♠ 6 5
                    ♡ 9 3
                    ◇ 9 6
                    ♣ A K 10 7 4 3 2
```

West	North	East	South
2 ♠	Dbl	4 ♠	5 ♣
P	6 ♣	All Pass	

Opening Lead: ♠ King

Declarer ruffed the opening lead and drew the outstanding trump. He took a diamond finesse. West won and returned a spade. Declarer ruffed, came to his hand and took a losing heart finesse. Down one.

Question: What was the biggest card in declarer's hand that was missed?

The other declarer claimed after the opening lead. What? Yes, what's the key card? The heart nine! Remember an early hand in this chapter?

In combination with the heart eight, after ruffing another spade, declarer can just lead a heart and cover West's card. East will be endplayed. A spade return is a ruff/sluff and anything else is a free finesse.

NO FINESSES, LET THE OPPONENTS DO THE WORK

♠ Q J 4 3
♡ 9 3
◇ A 10 2
♣ K J 4 2

♠ K 10 5   ♠ 9 7 6 2
♡ K Q J 8 4   ♡ 10 2
◇ Q 8 4   ◇ Q 9 7 6
♣ 9 3   ♣ 10 6 5

♠ A 8
♡ A 7 6 5
◇ K J 3
♣ A Q 8 7

South	West	North	East
1 ♣	1 ♡	Dbl	P
2 NT	P	3 NT	All Pass

Opening Lead: ♡ King

Declarer counted eight top tricks. He ducked the first trick, West continued with the heart jack. When East followed, declarer won. He took a diamond finesse into East; at least if it lost, East was out of hearts.

East won and returned a club. Declarer finished with the eight tricks he started with. If you took the diamond finesse the other way, you can see West had it too. Sorry, down one.

Question: What's the proper line of play? Yes, both East/West have the ◇ Q.

At the other table, as soon as the declarer saw East follow to the second heart, she knew no finesses were necessary. She won the second heart and played three rounds of clubs. When West showed out, declarer played a heart.

After taking his heart tricks, West had to give declarer a ninth trick. Declarer discarded carefully, keeping three diamonds and two spades. She had to discard a club, but dummy kept its club winner for later.

AVOIDING FINESSES: EASY ELIMINATION

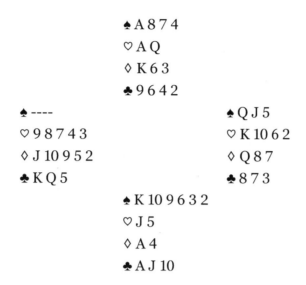

Contract: 4 ♠

Opening Lead: ◊ Jack

Declarer won the opening lead and cashed the A-K of trumps. Then our finesse addict played a heart to the queen. East won, cashed the high trump, and played a club. West won and played a diamond. Another club finesse meant down one.

Declarer lost two clubs, one heart, and one spade.

Question: How would a "non-finesse addict" play?

The other declarer (Remember I told you it's always good to be the 'other declarer') won the opening lead and cashed the A-K of trumps. She next played the diamond king and ruffed a diamond. Now showing her disdain for finesses, she played the heart ace, then the heart queen (another 'mirage').

Whoever won the heart was endplayed. If West, he had to lead a club or concede a ruff/sluff. If East, he could play a club, reaching the same ending.

Declarer lost one club, one heart, and one spade.

NO FINESSES: MULTIPLE ENDPLAYS ON THE BIDDING

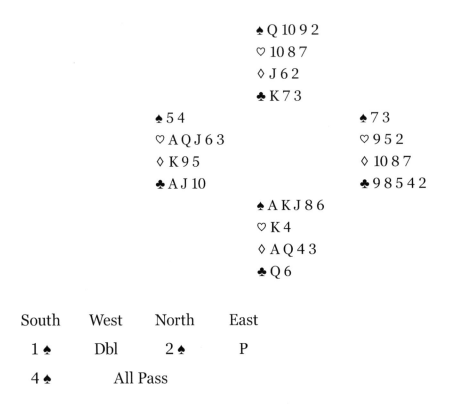

♠ Q 10 9 2
♡ 10 8 7
◊ J 6 2
♣ K 7 3

♠ 5 4
♡ A Q J 6 3
◊ K 9 5
♣ A J 10

♠ 7 3
♡ 9 5 2
◊ 10 8 7
♣ 9 8 5 4 2

♠ A K J 8 6
♡ K 4
◊ A Q 4 3
♣ Q 6

South	West	North	East
1 ♠	Dbl	2 ♠	P
4 ♠	All Pass		

Opening Lead: ♠ 4

Declarer won the opening lead and drew the last trumps. Both the bidding and opening lead suggested the contract was in jeopardy. Declarer tried a diamond finesse, losing to the king. West exited a diamond.

Declarer led a heart to the king. Down one, losing two hearts, one club, and one diamond.

Question: Given the bidding, how could declarer have done better?

Instead of all these optimistic finesses, which rate to lose, the other declarer led a small diamond towards the jack. West won and played a second trump. Declarer led a small club. West had to duck.

Declarer played three rounds of diamonds discarding a club from dummy, and exited a club. All the minors were stripped.

West was endplayed. Declarer's king of hearts had to score a trick.

LET DEFENDER RUFF TO BE ENDPLAYED

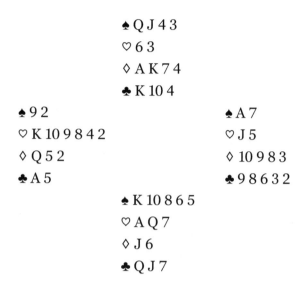

Contract: 4 ♠

Opening Lead: ♣ Ace

West led the club ace and continued a club. Declarer won and led a trump. East won the ace and gave West a club ruff. West exited a diamond. Declarer drew the last trump and took a heart finesse. Down one.

Question: Good opening lead or was there a better plan?

At the other table, the first two tricks were the same. However, before starting the trumps, declarer played the A-K of diamonds and ruffed a diamond.

Now he started the trumps. West ruffed a club but was endplayed. He had to either return a heart or give declarer a ruff/sluff.

4-1 SPLITS: FINESSE? SOMETHING ELSE?

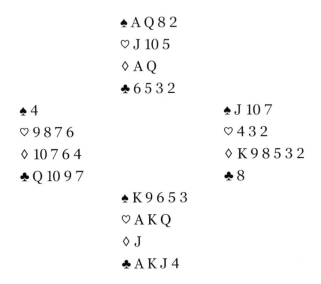

```
                    ♠ A Q 8 2
                    ♡ J 10 5
                    ♢ A Q
                    ♣ 6 5 3 2
         ♠ 4                         ♠ J 10 7
         ♡ 9 8 7 6                   ♡ 4 3 2
         ♢ 10 7 6 4                  ♢ K 9 8 5 3 2
         ♣ Q 10 9 7                  ♣ 8
                    ♠ K 9 6 5 3
                    ♡ A K Q
                    ♢ J
                    ♣ A K J 4
```

Contract: 6 ♠

Opening Lead: ♡ 9

Declarer won the opening lead and started trumps correctly by leading the king. He cashed the club ace, finished trumps ending in dummy and led a second club.

When East discarded, he won the club king and tried a diamond finesse to discard a club. East won, and declarer still had a club loser. Down one.

Question: Difficult, but if you think hand type, you will see your way home.

The declarer at the other table asked himself what could go wrong. Only 4-1 splits in a black suit. He started trumps by leading the king and drew the rest. But the clubs could wait. After drawing trumps, he set about elimination of the red suits. He cashed the diamond ace and ruffed a diamond. Then he cashed the other two high hearts. OK, the red suits were gone.

Now it was club time. He led the ace, then a low club. If clubs were 3-2, he could claim. If they were 4-1, whoever won the second club was endplayed; either a club away from the queen or a ruff/sluff.

106

AVOIDING A FINESSE BY COUNTING

```
                    ♠ A J 4 3
                    ♡ K 10 6 5
                    ◇ 6 4 2
                    ♣ A 10
        ♠ 10 8 6                        ♠ Q 9 7 2
        ♡ 3                             ♡ 8
        ◇ K J 9 8 7 5                   ◇ 10
        ♣ 8 6 4                         ♣ K Q J 9 7 5 3
                    ♠ K 5
                    ♡ A Q J 9 7 4 2
                    ◇ A Q 3
                    ♣ 2
```

East	South	West	North
3 ♣	4 ♡	P	6 ♡
	All Pass		

Opening Lead: ♣ 4

Declarer had two possible diamond losers, but had finesses in spades and diamonds, a 75% chance. After drawing trumps, he tried one, then the other. Down one.

Question: Was there any way to improve the odds?

Maybe. The other declarer played along elimination lines. He won the club ace, ruffed a club high, and drew trumps. He played the A-K of spades, and ruffed a spade, hoping to drop the queen. Nope.

East's distribution was 3-1-2-7 or 4-1-1-7. Declarer crossed to dummy with a trump and led the spade jack. If East showed out, declarer would discard a diamond, endplaying West.

If East had the spade queen, declarer would ruff and lead a low diamond endplaying whoever won the trick. Assuming East wins, he has to give declarer a ruff/sluff.

107

FINESSE? ELIMINATION AND ENDPLAY

```
                    ♠ A
                    ♡ K J 5 2
                    ◇ 7 6 4 3 2
                    ♣ A Q 3
    ♠ Q J 10 6                      ♠ 9 8 7 4 3
    ♡ 9 6                           ♡ 10 7
    ◇ A Q J                         ◇ 8 5
    ♣ 10 8 6 5                      ♣ K J 9 7
                    ♠ K 5 2
                    ♡ A Q 8 4 3
                    ◇ K 10 9
                    ♣ 4 2
```

Contract: 4 ♡

Opening Lead: ♠ Queen

Declarer won the opening lead and drew trumps. He led a diamond to the nine, losing to the jack. West shifted to a club. Declarer lost a club and two more diamonds. Down one.

Question: The other declarer made four hearts against good defense. How?

Hand pattern recognition. Lots of trumps in both hands think what? Elimination and end play, not a bunch of finesses.

After drawing trumps, she discarded a club on the spade king, ruffed her last spade, and then played ace and a club. No club finesse! The club queen is a 'mirage'; if it were a deuce, this line of play would have been more apparent.

Whoever won the club was endplayed. If West won, he had to play diamonds. If East won and played a diamond, declarer would cover the spot card, and now West would be endplayed. Have you noticed how many 'mirage' queens we have seen?

PARTIALLY AVOIDING ANOTHER FINESSE

```
                    ♠ A Q 10
                    ♡ A 4
                    ◇ J 7 4
                    ♣ 8 7 6 5 3
        ♠ 9 2                       ♠ 6 5 3
        ♡ 9 7 3 2                   ♡ J 10 8 5
        ◇ A K 10 5                  ◇ Q 8 6 3
        ♣ K Q 4                     ♣ 9 2
                    ♠ K J 8 7 4
                    ♡ K Q 6
                    ◇ 9 2
                    ♣ A J 10
```

West	North	East	South
1 ◇	P	P	1 ♠
P	2 ◇	P	2 ♡
P	3 ♠	P	4 ♠
	All Pass		

Opening Lead: ◇ Ace

Declarer ruffed the third round of diamonds, East playing the queen. Declarer knew from the bidding West held the K-Q of clubs. Since dummy only had three trumps, he drew trumps, and played the ace of clubs, hoping West had started with K-Q doubleton. Down one. At least it was a plan.

Question: Could you improve the plan? Clue: Maybe a different doubleton?

The other declarer saw one other chance. After ruffing the third diamond, he played a trump to the ace. Then he played three rounds of hearts. A trump to the queen was followed by a club finesse. West had a doubleton spade, declarer's hope, and was endplayed. A partial elimination.

If East was getting a club ruff, declarer was always going down. If West had the last trump to get out, declarer could hope for K-Q doubleton of clubs.

PARTIALLY AVOIDING A FINESSE

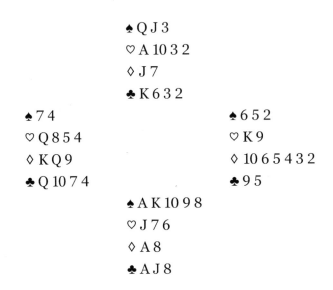

                    ♠ Q J 3
                    ♡ A 10 3 2
                    ◊ J 7
                    ♣ K 6 3 2
    ♠ 7 4   ♠ 6 5 2
    ♡ Q 8 5 4   ♡ K 9
    ◊ K Q 9   ◊ 10 6 5 4 3 2
    ♣ Q 10 7 4   ♣ 9 5
                    ♠ A K 10 9 8
                    ♡ J 7 6
                    ◊ A 8
                    ♣ A J 8

Contract: 4 ♠
Opening Lead: ◊ King

Declarer saw one diamond loser and a lot of finesse positions in hearts and clubs. He won the opening lead and started the guessing. All the finesses lost, both suits were 4-2, and when the smoke cleared, he was down one.

Question: Was there a better way to handle these combinations?

At the other table, declarer wished he had a fourth trump in dummy. Then an elimination play would be easy. But, hey, you've got what you've got.

He cashed only two rounds of trumps, to leave a trump in both hands and played a diamond. He was rewarded; West did not have a trump to return. West chose to break the club suit. Ten tricks.

If West had chosen hearts, South would have finessed, losing to East's king. But declarer could later finesse West's queen, a position he did not have earlier.

FINESSE? PARTIAL ELIMINATION & UNBLOCK

```
                    ♠ A K J
                    ♡ K 9 8 5 4
                    ◊ K 8
                    ♣ 9 7 5
    ♠ 10 8 5 4                      ♠ Q 9 3
    ♡ 3                             ♡ J 10
    ◊ 10 9 7 4                      ◊ A Q J 5 3
    ♣ 10 8 3 2                      ♣ Q J 6
                    ♠ 7 6 2
                    ♡ A Q 7 6 2
                    ◊ 6 2
                    ♣ A K 4
```

Contract: 4 ♡

Opening Lead: ◊ 10

East won the first two tricks and switched to a trump. Declarer drew trumps and trying to avoid the spade finesse, cashed the A-K of clubs and played another club. West shifted to a spade. Down one.

Question: How did the other declarer make four hearts?

Play was the same the first three tricks. Before drawing the last trump, declarer cashed the club ace. Why? To try to endplay East, if possible, to play a spade.

Did you notice above at the first table West switched to a spade? How did West get on lead after A-K of clubs and a club? Because East defended well. East could see the endplay coming, and unblocked the club Q-J under the A-K.

South should cash the club ace early. Do you think it will be as easy if before drawing all the trumps for East to see he must play the club queen under the ace? And the jack under the king?

A good declarer will make this play early in the hand, not at the end when everyone knows what is happening. Try to catch a defender napping.

AVOIDING A FINESSE THE BEST YOU CAN

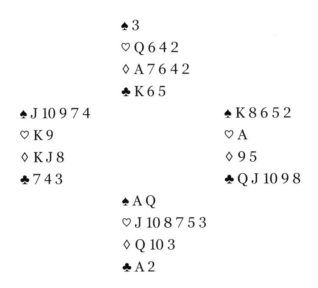

```
                        ♠ 3
                        ♡ Q 6 4 2
                        ◊ A 7 6 4 2
                        ♣ K 6 5
        ♠ J 10 9 7 4                      ♠ K 8 6 5 2
        ♡ K 9                             ♡ A
        ◊ K J 8                           ◊ 9 5
        ♣ 7 4 3                           ♣ Q J 10 9 8
                        ♠ A Q
                        ♡ J 10 8 7 5 3
                        ◊ Q 10 3
                        ♣ A 2
```

Contract: 4 ♡

Opening Lead: ♠ Jack

Declarer had two trump losers, barring an accident, and saw he would have to avoid losing two diamonds. After losing two rounds of trumps and the opponents returning clubs, he played a diamond to the ace, then a diamond to his queen. Down one.

Question: What are the opponents good for? Yes, breaking new suits for you.

The other declarer wanted to put the opponents to work. He saw he might not be able to avoid a diamond guess completely, but he could improve his chances. He won the opening lead and cashed another spade, discarding a club from dummy.

Then he played the A-K of clubs. With the black suits eliminated, he led the trump queen. East won the ace and played the diamond nine. This trick went nine, ten, jack, ace.

Declarer led another trump. West won and had no answer. He had to cash the diamond king, or give a ruff/sluff. Elimination, to whatever degree possible, always makes life more difficult for the opponents.

PARTIALLY AVOIDING A FINESSE

♠ 10 8 3
♡ 10 9 3
◊ A J 9 3
♣ A Q 8

♠ J 7 2   ♠ A K 9 6 4
♡ 7 5 4   ♡ J 2
◊ 8 7 5   ◊ K Q 4
♣ 10 9 5 2   ♣ 7 6 3

♠ Q 5
♡ A K Q 8 6
◊ 10 6 2
♣ K J 4

East	South	West	North
1 ♠	2 ♡	P	2 ♠
P	4 ♡	All Pass	

Opening Lead: ♠ 2

Declarer ruffed the third round of spades and drew trumps. He led a diamond to the jack. East won and returned a spade. Declarer ruffed and took another diamond finesse.

Down one. "Were you in the men's room during the bidding," asked North?

Question: What was North referring to? What other line of play was available?

East was a big favorite to hold both diamond honors. The other declarer tried for a partial elimination. After ruffing the third spade, he drew only two rounds of trumps and then cashed three rounds of clubs.

Now he was ready to take a diamond finesse. East won but had no safe exit, not having the last trump. He had to either lead away from his diamond honor or give up a ruff/sluff. Making four hearts.

NO FINESSE: AVOID BREAKING A SUIT

♠ A Q 7 5 2
♡ K 5 4
◊ A K 10 3
♣ Q

♠ 8   ♠ K J
♡ 10 2   ♡ A J 9 6
◊ J 7 2   ◊ Q 9 8 6 5
♣ A K 10 8 7 6 5   ♣ 4 2

♠ 10 9 6 4 3
♡ Q 8 7 3
◊ 4
♣ J 9 3

West	North	East	South
3 ♣	Dbl	P	3 ♠
P	4 ♠	All Pass	

Opening Lead: ♣ Ace

West switched to a diamond at trick two. Declarer won and ruffed a diamond. He led a spade to the queen. East won and returned a diamond. South drew trumps, but had to start the heart suit, losing two heart tricks. Down one.

Question: What was this hand all about?

The declarer at the other table wanted to avoid breaking the heart suit. Also, the trump finesse was probable a waste of time with West having the A-K of clubs.

He played a spade to the ace. He cashed the other high diamond, discarding a club, and ruffed the last diamond. He ruffed his last club. When East didn't overruff, declarer played a trump.

East was endplayed into starting the hearts.

114

FINESSES AVAILABLE: NO THANK YOU

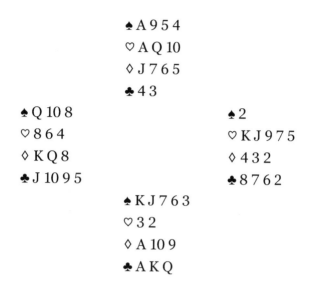

♠ A 9 5 4
♡ A Q 10
◊ J 7 6 5
♣ 4 3

♠ Q 10 8
♡ 8 6 4
◊ K Q 8
♣ J 10 9 5

♠ 2
♡ K J 9 7 5
◊ 4 3 2
♣ 8 7 6 2

♠ K J 7 6 3
♡ 3 2
◊ A 10 9
♣ A K Q

Contract: 4 ♠
Opening Lead: ♣ Jack

Declarer was faced with four possible losers if all the cards were lying badly. He won the opening lead and started trumps by leading the king to guard against 4-0 in either hand. Then a spade to the ace revealed a trump loser.

He took a diamond finesse, losing and West returned a club. He lost a heart finesse, then lost another diamond finesse. As feared, everything was lying badly. Down one.

Question: Do you remember the song "Everything Happens To Me"?

The other declarer, after two rounds of trumps, cashed the other two high clubs, discarding a low heart from dummy. Then he led the heart ace and the heart queen, another 'mirage'. East won and played a diamond. West won but was endplayed. Have you noticed how many queens we have sacrificed?

Had West won the heart king, he would have had to lead a diamond. The contract was guaranteed.

115

FINESSE: NOT THE ONE YOU MIGHT THINK

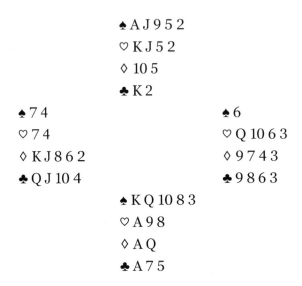

<pre>
                    ♠ A J 9 5 2
                    ♡ K J 5 2
                    ◊ 10 5
                    ♣ K 2
        ♠ 7 4   ♠ 6
        ♡ 7 4   ♡ Q 10 6 3
        ◊ K J 8 6 2   ◊ 9 7 4 3
        ♣ Q J 10 4   ♣ 9 8 6 3
                    ♠ K Q 10 8 3
                    ♡ A 9 8
                    ◊ A Q
                    ♣ A 7 5
</pre>

Contract: 6 ♠

Opening Lead: ♣ Queen

Declarer won the opening lead and drew trumps. He considered playing a heart to the jack. But if that lost and a diamond came back, he would be at a crossroads. If hearts were 3-3, he wouldn't need the diamond finesse.

Instead, he cashed the A-K of hearts and led a third heart towards the jack. West showed out, then the diamond finesse lost, down one.

"Both finesses were off anyhow, partner," said South. North was just shaking her head, trying not to say anything.

Question: What do you think North wanted to say?

The other declarer won the opening lead with the club king. After drawing trumps, he saw a more effective way to guarantee the contract, without either of the finesses the first declarer was thinking about.

He cashed the ace of clubs and ruffed a club. He played a low heart from dummy to his nine. If West had won the ten, he would have been endplayed in both red suits.

CAREFUL DISCARDING TO ENDPLAY DEFENDER

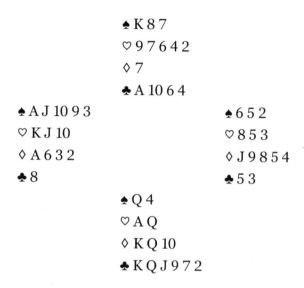

```
                    ♠ K 8 7
                    ♡ 9 7 6 4 2
                    ♦ 7
                    ♣ A 10 6 4
    ♠ A J 10 9 3                    ♠ 6 5 2
    ♡ K J 10                        ♡ 8 5 3
    ♦ A 6 3 2                       ♦ J 9 8 5 4
    ♣ 8                             ♣ 5 3
                    ♠ Q 4
                    ♡ A Q
                    ♦ K Q 10
                    ♣ K Q J 9 7 2
```

Contract: 5 ♣ (West opened 1 ♠)
Opening Lead: ♦ Ace

West led the diamond ace and continued another diamond. Declarer won, discarding a spade from dummy. After drawing trumps, declarer led a spade. West won and returned a spade.

Left to having to try the heart finesse, declarer was down one.

Question: Was there a way home? Could you have avoided the heart finesse?

What kind of hand is this? Lots of trumps, think endplay. It's a variation of a Morton's Fork. The other declarer discarded a heart from dummy on the second diamond at trick two, saving the third spade.

After drawing trumps, he also led a spade, but with three spades in dummy, West had to duck. If West had won, declarer would have discarded his heart queen on the spade king.

Then declarer came to his hand and now discarded a spade on his last high diamond. When he exited with the spade queen, West was endplayed. No heart finesse, thank you. Making five clubs.

TWO FINESSES OR SOMETHING ELSE

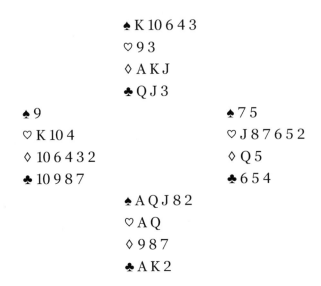

```
                        ♠ K 10 6 4 3
                        ♡ 9 3
                        ◇ A K J
                        ♣ Q J 3
        ♠ 9                             ♠ 7 5
        ♡ K 10 4                        ♡ J 8 7 6 5 2
        ◇ 10 6 4 3 2                    ◇ Q 5
        ♣ 10 9 8 7                      ♣ 6 5 4
                        ♠ A Q J 8 2
                        ♡ A Q
                        ◇ 9 8 7
                        ♣ A K 2
```

Contract: 6 ♠

Opening Lead: ♣ 10

Declarer won the opening lead. It appeared that success depended on one of two red suit finesses. After drawing trumps, declarer tried one, then the other. Down one.

Question: Was there any way to increase declarer's chances?

After the same start, the other declarer, saw that if the diamond finesse was working, he could guarantee his contract and protect against a doubleton queen with East.

After drawing trumps, he cashed two more rounds of clubs, then cashed the A-K of diamonds. He planned to give West a diamond and West would be endplayed. If East won the third diamond, he would have the heart finesse as a LAST RESORT.

He was rewarded when East's doubleton queen of diamonds fell.

NO FINESSES: ENDPLAY

```
                    ♠ K Q J 5
                    ♡ A 8 6
                    ◊ 8 5 2
                    ♣ 10 5 4
    ♠ 10 7                         ♠ 8 6 4 3
    ♡ Q 9 3                        ♡ 10 7 4
    ◊ K 4 3                        ◊ J 10 9 7
    ♣ K Q J 9 3                    ♣ 8 7
                    ♠ A 9 2
                    ♡ K J 5 2
                    ◊ A Q 6
                    ♣ A 6 2
```

Contract: 3 NT

Opening Lead: ♣ King

Declarer counted eight winners. There were two finesses in the red suits. If either was successful, a ninth trick was available. He ducked the first club. When East followed to the second club, declarer formed a new plan. Since West had only a five-card suit, declarer thought about an endplay.

He won the second club and cashed four rounds of spades. He played a club, thinking, "I've got West now, he will have to play a red suit." But as West cashed the clubs, declarer realized he had squeezed his own hand. On the last club, he had to reduce his hand to ♠ --- ♡ K J ◊ A Q ◊ ---.

West exited a heart and declarers heart honors became two tricks instead of three, the dummy having ♡ A 8 6. He won in dummy and tried the diamond finesse, down one.

Question: What happened? Wasn't declarer on the right road to success?

The other declarer saw the ending. The fourth spade could wait and the same plan was a success. The remaining hearts were ♡ A 8 6 in dummy and ♡ K J 5 in hand. West was endplayed but declarer scored three heart tricks.

FINESSES CAN WAIT, HIGH CARDS DON'T GO AWAY

```
                        ♠ A Q J
                        ♡ 9 7 2
                        ◊ Q 9 7
                        ♣ J 7 5 4
        ♠ 7 6 4 3                        ♠ K 8 2
        ♡ 10 8 4 3                       ♡ A K Q 6 5
        ◊ 6 2                            ◊ 4 3
        ♣ 10 6 2                         ♣ Q 9 8
                        ♠ 10 9 5
                        ♡ J
                        ◊ A K J 10 8 5
                        ♣ A K 3
```

South	West	North	East
1 ◊	P	1 NT	2 ♡
3 ◊	4 ♡	5 ◊	All Pass

Opening Lead: ♡ 3

Declarer ruffed the second round of hearts and drew trumps. He took a spade finesse, losing and East returned another heart. Declarer ruffed and ran his tricks. East saved three clubs to the queen. Down one.

Question: Was there a way to avoid this finesse?

Maybe. The great columnist and expert Frank Stewart recently discussed this theme. "A finesse that will win now will win later,,,,,,, a missing honor won't magically change hands."

The other declarer, having read all of Frank's great books, was in no rush to finesse. After drawing trumps, he ruffed dummy's last heart, cashed the A-K of clubs and led a third club.

When East won, he was endplayed. If he led a spade, declarer would win and discard his other spade on the last club. If East led a heart, declarer would discard a spade from hand, ruff in dummy and discard another spade on the last good club. Thanks, Frank.

NO FINESSES: LET THEM START THE "IFFY" SUIT

$\spadesuit$ A 10 7 6
$\heartsuit$ K 3 2
$\diamond$ A 6 2
$\clubsuit$ J 6 3

$\spadesuit$ 3 $\spadesuit$ 4 2
$\heartsuit$ Q 9 5 $\heartsuit$ 10 8 7 6
$\diamond$ Q J 10 9 7 5 $\diamond$ K 8 4
$\clubsuit$ A 8 2 $\clubsuit$ Q 10 9 7

$\spadesuit$ K Q J 9 8 5
$\heartsuit$ A J 4
$\diamond$ 3
$\clubsuit$ K 5 4

West	North	East	South
2 $\diamond$	P	3 $\diamond$	3 $\spadesuit$
P	4 $\spadesuit$	All Pass	

Opening Lead: $\diamond$ Queen

Declarer won the opening lead and drew trumps. He played a club to his king, losing to West's ace. A diamond came back. Declarer ruffed and led a club to dummy's jack. Of course, that lost to the queen.

After losing three club tricks, he took a losing heart finesse. Down one.

Question: Was declarer unlucky, or did he deserve to go down?

The first declarer took the three finesse road, but there was a 100% road he overlooked (a nice way of saying he went down in a cold contract).

At the other table, with an "iffy" side suit like the clubs, the idea is to force the opponents to lead the suit first. He won the diamond ace and ruffed a diamond. He played a trump to dummy, ruffed the last diamond and drew the last trump.

Now he cashed the A-K of hearts and played a heart. One of the opponents had to start the "iffy" suit, clubs. By forcing a club play, he could not lose more than two club tricks. He lost two clubs and one heart, no finesses.

FINESSE? WHY BOTHER?

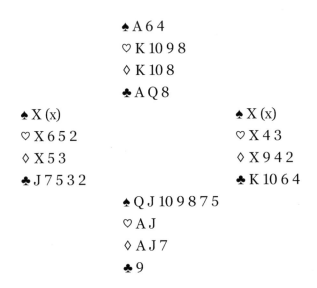

```
                    ♠ A 6 4
                    ♡ K 10 9 8
                    ◇ K 10 8
                    ♣ A Q 8
     ♠ X (x)                          ♠ X (x)
     ♡ X 6 5 2                        ♡ X 4 3
     ◇ X 5 3                          ◇ X 9 4 2
     ♣ J 7 5 3 2                      ♣ K 10 6 4
                    ♠ Q J 10 9 8 7 5
                    ♡ A J
                    ◇ A J 7
                    ♣ 9
```

Contract: 6 ♠

Opening Lead: ♣ 3

So many finesses, where to start? (Yes, West might have 14 cards). At the first table, declarer won the club ace, ruffed a club, and took a losing trump finesse. He later misguessed the heart queen, down one.

Question: Unlucky or misplayed?

Why are you taking any finesses? Just because you can? The way to assure this contract is to take no finesses. At the other table, the declarer won the opening lead and ruffed a club. He cashed the trump ace and ruffed another club. Then he played a trump. Game, set, and match.

Whoever won the trump king had to lead a red suit, guessing that queen for him, or lead a club, conceding a ruff/sluff.

Finesses are useful, but experts use them only as a LAST RESORT.

DELAYING THE FINESSE

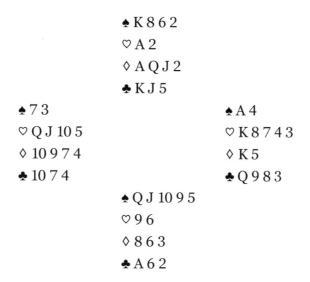

```
                    ♠ K 8 6 2
                    ♡ A 2
                    ◊ A Q J 2
                    ♣ K J 5
    ♠ 7 3                              ♠ A 4
    ♡ Q J 10 5                         ♡ K 8 7 4 3
    ◊ 10 9 7 4                         ◊ K 5
    ♣ 10 7 4                           ♣ Q 9 8 3
                    ♠ Q J 10 9 5
                    ♡ 9 6
                    ◊ 8 6 3
                    ♣ A 6 2
```

Contract: 4 ♠

Opening Lead: ♡ Queen

The first declarer won the opening lead and started the trumps. East won the spade ace, cashed the heart king and returned a trump. Declarer won in hand and took a diamond finesse. East won the king and returned a diamond.

Since the diamonds were 4-2, declarer needed the club finesse. Down one.

Question. Unlucky, or in too much of a hurry to take the diamond finesse?

Declarer could be forgiven for relying on the club or diamond finesse, or 3-3 diamonds. But there was no rush to take the diamond finesse. The other declarer cashed the diamond ace first, then came to hand with the club ace and led a diamond to the queen.

East won the king and was endplayed. Returning a heart or club would give declarer the contract, a ruff/sluff or a free finesse.

This declarer realized that if the diamond finesse was going to succeed, there was no rush to take it. He had enough entries to lead twice towards the Q J and get a discard for his club loser. The club finesse was a backup plan if needed as a LAST RESORT.

ONE FINESSE OK, BUT THAT'S ENOUGH: ENDPLAY

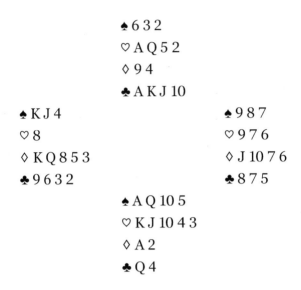

```
              ♠ 6 3 2
              ♡ A Q 5 2
              ◊ 9 4
              ♣ A K J 10
♠ K J 4                        ♠ 9 8 7
♡ 8                            ♡ 9 7 6
◊ K Q 8 5 3                    ◊ J 10 7 6
♣ 9 6 3 2                      ♣ 8 7 5
              ♠ A Q 10 5
              ♡ K J 10 4 3
              ◊ A 2
              ♣ Q 4
```

Contract: 6 ♡

Opening Lead: ◊ King

Declarer won the opening lead and drew trumps. He cashed the high clubs, discarding the diamond loser and a spade. He led a spade to his ten. West won and safely exited a diamond. Declarer ruffed, returned to dummy for another spade finesse. Down one.

Question: How could declarer have made six hearts without all these finesses?

The other declarer won the opening lead and cashed the K-J of trumps. He played three rounds of clubs discarding a diamond. He then made the key play, he ruffed dummy's remaining diamond.

Now it was time to draw the last trump with the queen, cash another club, and play a spade. West will win but has no safe exit, the diamonds having also been eliminated.

ELIMINATION PROVIDES TWO
FINESSES INSTEAD OF ONE

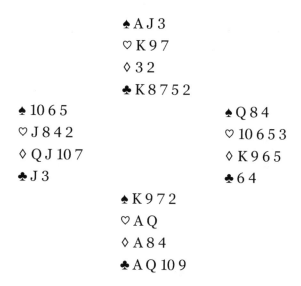

♠ A J 3
♡ K 9 7
◊ 3 2
♣ K 8 7 5 2

♠ 10 6 5
♡ J 8 4 2
◊ Q J 10 7
♣ J 3

♠ Q 8 4
♡ 10 6 5 3
◊ K 9 6 5
♣ 6 4

♠ K 9 7 2
♡ A Q
◊ A 8 4
♣ A Q 10 9

Contract: 6 ♣

Opening Lead: ◊ Queen

Declarer won the opening lead and drew trumps. He tried to set up the spades to discard a diamond. He played a spade to the jack. Down one.

Question: How would you have improved declarer's chances?

At the other table, declarer thought about putting the defenders to work. After drawing trumps, he cashed the A-Q of hearts, and went to dummy with a trump. He discarded a diamond on the heart king and played a diamond.

If East won, the hand was over. Assuming West won and started the spades, declarer would play low, not the jack. If East played low or had the queen but no ten, declarer was home. If he played the ten, declarer still had a finesse to try for the queen.

So many better chances than an early finesse of the jack.

LOTS OF THIS AND THAT

BUT ON THE OTHER HAND__

```
                    ♠ 8 3
                    ♡ J 4
                    ◊ A J 9 8 7 3
                    ♣ J 8 2
   ♠ K 10 6 5 2                      ♠ J 9 4
   ♡ Q 8 3 2                         ♡ K 9 7 6
   ◊ 6 4                             ◊ Q 5 2
   ♣ K 3                             ♣ Q 6 5
                    ♠ A Q 7
                    ♡ A 10 5
                    ◊ K 10
                    ♣ A 10 9 7 4
```

Contract: 3 NT

Opening Lead: ♠ 5

Declarer won the spade queen. Remembering from my book about cashing the long suit, she played the king, then the ace of diamonds. Nothing good happened ☹.

She now switched to Plan B, club finesses, leading the eight. West won the king and continued with the spade king. Declarer ducked, won the next spade and tried the ace of clubs. No queen ☹. Eight tricks, down one.

Question: What happened to those principles of two suits we were discussing?

Bridge is a hand, not a suit or two suits. This hand has entry problems. At the other table, the declarer led the diamond ten at trick two to dummy's jack.

What could East do? If he took the diamond queen, declarer had five diamond tricks, for a total of nine tricks. So he ducked. Declarer changed to plan B, two club finesses, but she had a second entry.

She led the club eight, and later overtook the diamond king, to repeat the club finesse. She took four clubs, two diamonds, two spades and one heart.

DRAWING TRUMPS: FINESSE?

```
                    ♠ 6 3
                    ♡ A Q 8 5 2
                    ◊ 7 6 3
                    ♣ A Q J
        ♠ Q 10 9                    ♠ 5 2
        ♡ K 9 7 6                   ♡ J 10 4
        ◊ Q J 10                    ◊ A 9 5 2
        ♣ 8 3 2                     ♣ 10 9 5 4
                    ♠ A K J 8 7 4
                    ♡ 3
                    ◊ K 8 4
                    ♣ K 7 6
```

Contract: 4 ♠

Opening Lead: ◊ Queen

East encouraged at trick one and declarer won the king. He went to dummy with a club and took a trump finesse. West won the queen and continued with the diamond jack and then the diamond ten.

East overtook to play the thirteenth diamond. This promoted West's ♠ 10 9 to the setting trick. Down one.

Question: Unavoidable? Was there a better line of play?

The other declarer counted ten tricks if trumps were 3-2. If they were 4-1, the heart finesse was a LAST RESORT.

He cashed the A-K of trumps. No finesses needed.

FINESSE? WHAT'S THE HURRY?

```
                    ♠ A 10 5
                    ♡ 7 3
                    ◇ K Q J 5 2
                    ♣ 10 7 4
    ♠ Q 6                          ♠ 9 8 7 3 2
    ♡ K Q J 9 4                    ♡ 10 8 5
    ◇ 8 7 3                        ◇ A 6
    ♣ K 8 6                        ♣ 9 5 2
                    ♠ K J 4
                    ♡ A 6 2
                    ◇ 10 9 4
                    ♣ A Q J 3
```

Contract: 3 NT
Opening Lead: ♡ King

Declarer won the third round of hearts and started diamonds. He was fortunate East had the diamond ace, but when East returned a club, declarer tried a finesse.

He lost four hearts, one club, and one diamond. Down two.

Question: Was there any road to nine tricks?

At the other table, play started the same, but declarer won the club ace, refusing the finesse. He cashed four rounds of diamonds, putting West under pressure. West was forced to discard a low spade and club.

Now declarer started spades, cashing the ace, planning to take a finesse. But a good thing happened on the way to the dummy. Up came the spade queen. Now declarer had nine tricks. Three spades, one heart, four diamonds, and one club.

NO FINESSE NEEDED, BUT I'M TAKING ONE

```
                    ♠ A Q 5
                    ♡ Q 9 7 3
                    ◇ J 10 3
                    ♣ 7 4 2
        ♠ K J 10 6              ♠ 9 8 7 4 2
        ♡ 8 2                   ♡ 6 4
        ◇ A K Q 8               ◇ 7 6 5 4
        ♣ K Q 8                 ♣ 6 3
                    ♠ 3
                    ♡ A K J 10 5
                    ◇ 9 2
                    ♣ A J 10 9 5
```

South	West	North	East
1 ♡	Dbl	2 ♡	P
3 ♣	P	4 ♡	P
P	Dbl	All Pass	

Opening Lead: ◇ King

Declarer ruffed the third diamond. He went to dummy and took a club finesse. West won and returned a spade. After drawing trumps, declarer lost another club finesse. Down one.

Question: Given the bidding, do you see a plan to make four hearts?

At the other table, declarer reasoned correctly all the missing high cards were with West. What kind of hand was this? Lots of trumps in both hands, think elimination and endplay.

The diamonds were gone, now it's a matter of getting rid of the spades. Being short on entries, declarer took an unnecessary spade finesse, cashed the spade ace and ruffed a spade.

The stage was set. After drawing trumps, when West won a club, he was endplayed. Sometimes it pays to take an 'unnecessary' but necessary finesse.

NO FINESSES (PESSIMIST), ALL
THE FINESSES (OPTIMIST)

```
                      ♠ A J 9 5 2
                      ♡ Q J 10 9 7
                      ◊ 9 6 5
                      ♣ ----
       ♠ 4                              ♠ K 8 7 6 3
       ♡ K 3                            ♡ 5
       ◊ K Q 7 3                        ◊ J 10 8
       ♣ A K 8 5 4 2                    ♣ J 9 7 3
                      ♠ Q 10
                      ♡ A 8 6 4 2
                      ◊ A 4 2
                      ♣ Q 10 6
```

South	West	North	East
1 ♡	2 ♣	4 ♣	P
4 ♡	All Pass		

Opening Lead: ♣ Ace

Declarer ruffed the opening lead. This declarer was the optimist. He took a heart finesse. West won the king and switched to the diamond king. Declarer won and after drawing the last trump, had to take a spade finesse.

East won and the defense cashed two diamond tricks. Unlucky, zero for two. Down one.

Question: Were you the optimist or the pessimist? How did you play?

At the other table, this declarer was the pessimist. He lost no finesses because he didn't take any. He played a trump to his ace. Then he played a spade to the ace and led another spade.

Now there were good spades in dummy to discard diamond losers. East could win the spade king, but had no winning options. West would win his trump trick while declarer was discarding losers on the spades.

131

WHICH FINESSE? HOW ABOUT NO FINESSES?

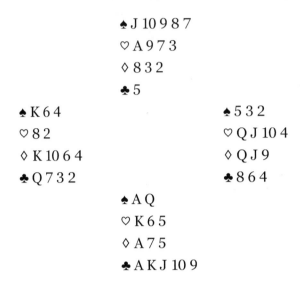

                    ♠ J 10 9 8 7
                    ♡ A 9 7 3
                    ◊ 8 3 2
                    ♣ 5
    ♠ K 6 4   ♠ 5 3 2
    ♡ 8 2   ♡ Q J 10 4
    ◊ K 10 6 4   ◊ Q J 9
    ♣ Q 7 3 2   ♣ 8 6 4
                    ♠ A Q
                    ♡ K 6 5
                    ◊ A 7 5
                    ♣ A K J 10 9

Contract: 3 NT
Opening Lead: ◊ 4

Declarer saw extra tricks in spades and clubs, but seeing them and getting them were two different things. With only one dummy entry, the spade finesse was not appealing. Declarer tried the ace, then queen of spades, no king appeared.

So he went to dummy and tried a club finesse. Declarer lost three diamonds, one club, and the spade king. Good try, bad result

Question: Was there a line of play that would assure nine tricks?

At the other table, declarer made a better offer. She won the third round of diamonds, East following to all three. So diamonds were 4-3. Now she led the spade queen, not the ace. The defense was helpless.

If West took the king, declarer had four spade tricks along with her other five. If West refused, declarer would go after clubs and have nine tricks: two spades, two hearts, one diamond, and four clubs. Sort of an 'anti-finesse' play.

RESISTING TEMPTATION (BY EDDIE KANTAR, JULY 2008)

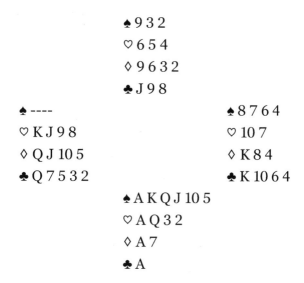

```
                  ♠ 9 3 2
                  ♡ 6 5 4
                  ◊ 9 6 3 2
                  ♣ J 9 8
   ♠ ----                        ♠ 8 7 6 4
   ♡ K J 9 8                     ♡ 10 7
   ◊ Q J 10 5                    ◊ K 8 4
   ♣ Q 7 5 3 2                   ♣ K 10 6 4
                  ♠ A K Q J 10 5
                  ♡ A Q 3 2
                  ◊ A 7
                  ♣ A
```

Contract: 4 ♠

Opening Lead: ◊ Queen

Declarer won the opening lead. With nine top tricks, a tenth trick could come from a successful heart finesse or a heart ruff. Declarer led a trump to dummy's nine and took a heart finesse.

West won and continued diamonds. Declarer ruffed the next diamond and continued his plan to ruff a heart, by playing the heart ace and more hearts. He finally ruffed a heart, but East overruffed. Down one.

Question: Did it matter who had the heart king?

No. This was another 'queen mirage'. Declarer had ten sure tricks no matter who had the heart king. The other declarer started by playing ace and a heart.

No matter what the opponents did, declarer could not be prevented from ruffing his last heart with the nine of trumps for his tenth trick.

TWO - WAY FINESSE? OTHER OPTION FIRST

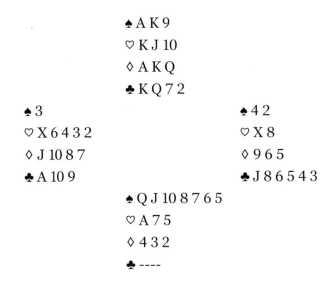

```
                        ♠ A K 9
                        ♡ K J 10
                        ◇ A K Q
                        ♣ K Q 7 2
        ♠ 3                                 ♠ 4 2
        ♡ X 6 4 3 2                         ♡ X 8
        ◇ J 10 8 7                          ◇ 9 6 5
        ♣ A 10 9                            ♣ J 8 6 5 4 3
                        ♠ Q J 10 8 7 6 5
                        ♡ A 7 5
                        ◇ 4 3 2
                        ♣ ----
```

Contract: 7 ♠ (A little pushy but)

Opening Lead: ♠ 3

Declarer won the opening lead and drew trumps. He played a few cards, but with not much to go on, decided to play____ for the heart queen. Down one.

Question: A 50/50 guess? A club or heart lead would have made life easier.

At the other table, declarer wasn't ready to put everything on a heart guess. There was an extra chance after the same lead. After drawing trumps, he led the club king. East played low.

Declarer ruffed, went to dummy with a diamond and ruffed another club. He returned to dummy and ruffed a third club. Voila! The club ace fell. Hand over!

And if it had not fallen? Back to square one. Try to guess the heart queen.

AVOIDING A FINESSE: A 'DUMMY REVERSAL'

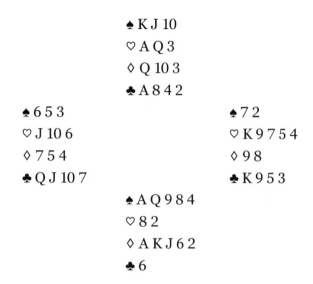

```
                      ♠ K J 10
                      ♡ A Q 3
                      ◊ Q 10 3
                      ♣ A 8 4 2
        ♠ 6 5 3                        ♠ 7 2
        ♡ J 10 6                       ♡ K 9 7 5 4
        ◊ 7 5 4                        ◊ 9 8
        ♣ Q J 10 7                     ♣ K 9 5 3
                      ♠ A Q 9 8 4
                      ♡ 8 2
                      ◊ A K J 6 2
                      ♣ 6
```

Contract: 7 ♠

Opening Lead: ♣ Queen

Declarer won the opening lead and drew trumps. Counting twelve tricks and without much thought, declarer took a heart finesse. Sure, swift, and wrong. Down one.

Question: Was there a better line of play rather than a 50/50 finesse?

At the other table, declarer won the club ace and ruffed a club. He cashed the A-K of trumps and ruffed another club. He led a diamond to dummy and ruffed the last club.

He played a heart to the ace, no finesse, thank you, and drew the last trump. He took the rest of the tricks with the good diamonds.

Had the trumps divided 4-1, the heart finesse was there as a LAST RESORT.

NO FINESSE, JUST RUFF IN DUMMY

```
                          ♠ Q 7 3 2
                          ♡ Q 2
                          ◊ K J 3
                          ♣ A 8 7 2
        ♠ A K J 10 6 5                    ♠ 8 4
        ♡ 4                               ♡ 8 7 6 3
        ◊ 9 7                             ◊ Q 10 5 4
        ♣ K Q 10 4                        ♣ 9 5 3
                          ♠ 9
                          ♡ A K J 10 9 5
                          ◊ A 8 6 2
                          ♣ J 6
```

South	West	North	East
1 ♡	1 ♠	2 NT	P
4 ♡	All Pass		

Opening Lead: ♠ Ace

West led the spade ace and switched to the club king. Declarer won and counted nine top tricks. He saw a tenth trick in diamonds, either by finessing the jack, or cashing the A-K of diamonds and leading to the jack. In the latter case, if West had the queen or the suit divided 3-3, he had his tenth trick.

He drew trumps and tried one of the diamond plays. Good operation in theory but the patient died. Down one.

Question: How did the other declarer handle the diamonds to make four hearts?

At the other table, the first two tricks were the same. Declarer took a simple approach having been given an opportunity by the defense (no trump switch, not so easy from West's hand).

Declarer simply played three rounds of diamonds, not caring what happened. He could not be prevented from ruffing a diamond in dummy with the queen of trumps for a tenth trick.

136

NO FINESSES: ANOTHER "QUEEN MIRAGE"

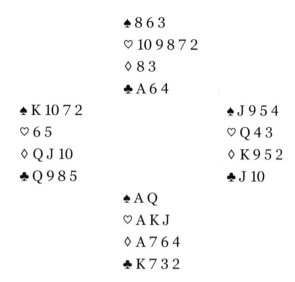

♠ 8 6 3
♥ 10 9 8 7 2
♦ 8 3
♣ A 6 4

♠ K 10 7 2
♥ 6 5
♦ Q J 10
♣ Q 9 8 5

♠ J 9 5 4
♥ Q 4 3
♦ K 9 5 2
♣ J 10

♠ A Q
♥ A K J
♦ A 7 6 4
♣ K 7 3 2

Contract: 3 ♥

Opening Lead: ♦ Queen

Declarer won the opening lead. Two possible finesses but only one entry. He cashed the A-K of the longer trump suit then went to dummy and took a spade finesse. West won and played a diamond. East won and cashed the trump queen.

Declarer still had to lose one diamond, one club, and one more spade. Down one.

Question: Was there a way to avoid one of these losers?

The queen of spades is a "mirage"; we have seen this on other hands. How would you play this hand if the spade queen were a deuce?

The other declarer won the opening lead. He played the spade ace, then the spade queen. He used his one entry to play a spade from the board and trump it in his hand. He lost one trick in each suit. Nine tricks, no finesses.

FINESSES? NO, AFTER YOU PLEASE

```
                    ♠ Q 6 3
                    ♡ A Q 6
                    ◇ K 9 7 2
                    ♣ 7 5 3
        ♠ 9 8 5                      ♠ K J 7 4 2
        ♡ K 10 9 2                   ♡ 7 3
        ◇ 8 5 4                      ◇ 10 6
        ♣ A Q 6                      ♣ 10 9 8 2
                    ♠ A 10
                    ♡ J 8 5 4
                    ◇ A Q J 3
                    ♣ K J 4
```

Contract: 3 NT
Opening Lead: ♡ 2

Declarer won the opening lead in his hand with the eight. He led a heart to dummy, winning the queen. Searching for a ninth trick, he started the clubs. West won and played another heart.

Declarer tried a club again. The defense won four clubs and one heart.

Question: Good start, bad finish. Was there a better way to find a ninth trick?

The other declarer saw the spades and clubs as "iffy" suits, the type you don't want to lead first. Believing the opening lead to be from a four-card suit, the first two tricks were the same. But the other declarer cashed the heart ace and played four rounds of diamonds.

He exited with the heart jack. West had to start one of the "iffy" suits. Declarer was assured of a ninth trick.

COMBINING YOUR CHANCES

Here is a hand Frank Stewart showed a few years ago in his excellent column. He had received another letter from the Society of Finessers complaining that his finesses never seem to work. They wrote, "Sir: We ...protest your disdain for finesses...You are in contempt of the percentages."

Frank wrote, "The Society won't like today's deal."

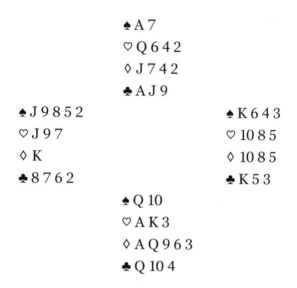

Contract: 3 NT

Opening Lead: ♠ 5

Declarer played low, East won and returned a spade. Declarer took a diamond finesse. West won and cashed the spades. Down one.

Frank pointed out to the Society that declarer can combine his chances by testing the hearts first. When hearts are 3-3, with two other suits for tricks, first cash the ace of the long one, then finesse in the other.

Declarer is rewarded when the diamond king falls. If not, he would try the clubs hoping for three clubs, four hearts, one spade and one diamond.

If hearts were 4-2, declarer would need diamond tricks and try the finesse. Thanks, Frank.

ONLY ONE FINESSE? TAKE AN EXTRA ONE, WHY NOT

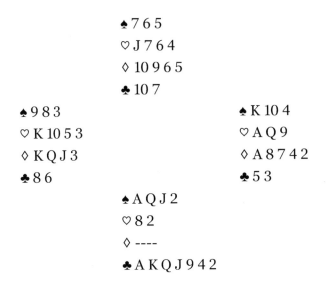

```
                    ♠ 7 6 5
                    ♡ J 7 6 4
                    ◊ 10 9 6 5
                    ♣ 10 7
        ♠ 9 8 3                    ♠ K 10 4
        ♡ K 10 5 3                 ♡ A Q 9
        ◊ K Q J 3                  ◊ A 8 7 4 2
        ♣ 8 6                      ♣ 5 3
                    ♠ A Q J 2
                    ♡ 8 2
                    ◊ ----
                    ♣ A K Q J 9 4 2
```

Contract: 5 ♣

Opening Lead: ♡ 3

Declarer ruffed the third heart. He played a club to the ten and took a spade finesse. He drew trumps and cashed the spade ace.

When the king did not fall, he was down one.

Question: Was there any chance to make this contract?

Slim, but slim is better than none. Think positive. The other declarer tried to imagine a position he needed. To start with, East had to have ♠ K x x.

And he needed to reach dummy twice to repeat the spade finesse. So declarer would have to take an extra finesse, a club to the seven.

Well, what do you know? Making five clubs.

WHICH FINESSE? BOTH OR MAYBE NEITHER

```
                    ♠ 10 5
                    ♡ K 8 2
                    ◊ 8 6 5
                    ♣ A 9 6 4 2
   ♠ 7 4                              ♠ 8 6 2
   ♡ Q 10 5 3                         ♡ 9 7 6 4
   ◊ J 10 9                           ◊ Q 7 3 2
   ♣ K 10 7 3                         ♣ J 8
                    ♠ A K Q J 9 3
                    ♡ A J
                    ◊ A K 4
                    ♣ Q 5
```

Contract: 6 ♠

Opening Lead: ◊ Jack

Declarer could count eleven tricks. He saw two possible finesses. He could lead a club to his queen. If East had the king, the club queen would probably make twelve tricks. If it lost, he was not down yet.

He could still finesse the jack of hearts. Neither of these lines were very good and each had flaws. But both failed. Down one.

Question: Was there a third line of play with a better chance of success?

The other declarer was not so in love with her club queen. She saw a second suit in dummy and at trick two played a low club from each hand. East won and returned a diamond. Declarer won and cashed the ace of trumps. She played a club to the ace and ruffed a club high.

If clubs were 3-3, the clubs were good. If necessary, declarer had the entries to ruff one more club and use the last club to discard her diamond. This line of play was about 84%, losing only if clubs were 5-1.

The club queen was another 'mirage'. If it had been a deuce, this line would have been more obvious.

WHICH FINESSE? NONE, THANK YOU

$$\spadesuit\ 9\ 8\ 5\ 4\ 3$$
$$\heartsuit\ 9\ 2$$
$$\diamondsuit\ A\ K\ Q\ 5$$
$$\clubsuit\ 7\ 6$$

$\spadesuit$ A Q 10 7 $\spadesuit$ J 2
$\heartsuit$ 10 8 7 3 $\heartsuit$ K 5
$\diamondsuit$ 8 3 $\diamondsuit$ J 10 9 4
$\clubsuit$ K J 8 $\clubsuit$ 10 9 4 3 2

$$\spadesuit\ K\ 6$$
$$\heartsuit\ A\ Q\ J\ 6\ 4$$
$$\diamondsuit\ 7\ 6\ 2$$
$$\clubsuit\ A\ Q\ 5$$

Contract: 3 NT
Opening Lead: $\heartsuit$ 3

South opened 1 NT and reached 3 NT. At trick one, East played the king, declarer won the ace. Declarer counted a likely eight tricks, with a possible ninth trick in clubs, diamonds, or spades. He tried the diamonds first, but they were 4-2. He led a spade to his king.

West won the ace, cashed two more spade tricks, and exited the heart ten. Declarer finished with the eight tricks he started with.

"The club finesse was offside too, partner," offered South as an excuse. North was not interested, being busy writing lose 10 IMPS.

Question: South lost his way. There was a sure road to 3 NT. Do you see it?

The other declarer decided to put the opponents to work rather than take any finesses. After testing the diamonds, he played off his high hearts. After West won the fourth heart, he was endplayed.

He had to lead a club or a spade, giving declarer a ninth trick. No finesses, thank you.

TAKE A FINESSE? IT'S ANOTHER 'MIRAGE'

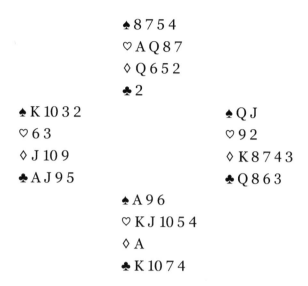

```
                    ♠ 8 7 5 4
                    ♡ A Q 8 7
                    ◇ Q 6 5 2
                    ♣ 2
   ♠ K 10 3 2                      ♠ Q J
   ♡ 6 3                           ♡ 9 2
   ◇ J 10 9                        ◇ K 8 7 4 3
   ♣ A J 9 5                       ♣ Q 8 6 3
                    ♠ A 9 6
                    ♡ K J 10 5 4
                    ◇ A
                    ♣ K 10 7 4
```

Contract: 4 ♡

Opening Lead: ◇ Jack

Declarer won the opening lead in hand perforce. He went to dummy with a trump to lead a club, planning to ruff clubs in dummy. West won the ace and returned a trump.

Declarer successfully ruffed two clubs but only had nine tricks. Down one.

Question: Was there a better line of play?

The first declarer had blinders on. The club king was a 'mirage' king. If the club king had been a deuce, how would he have played?

Like the other declarer who treated his clubs like four small and just led a low club from his hand at trick two. He won the trump return, but guess how many clubs he ruffed in dummy?

He won five hearts in hand, three ruffs, and two aces. Making four hearts.

143

ONE, TWO, OR NO FINESSES?

```
                    ♠ Q 9 8 2
                    ♡ 9 3
                    ♢ Q J 6 2
                    ♣ K Q 4
        ♠ 5                         ♠ 6 4
        ♡ A K J 8 4                 ♡ 10 7 6 5 2
        ♢ K 10 8 5                  ♢ 9 7 3
        ♣ 6 5 2                     ♣ A J 10
                    ♠ A K J 10 7 3
                    ♡ Q
                    ♢ A 4
                    ♣ 9 8 7 3
```

West	North	East	South
1 ♡	P	2 ♡	2 ♠
P	4 ♠	All Pass	

Opening Lead: ♡ Ace

West led the A-K of hearts (not best) and declarer ruffed the second round. After drawing trumps, declarer led a club to the king. East won and returned a club. Declarer took a diamond finesse, down one, losing one heart, two clubs, and one diamond.

Question: Did declarer give this much thought, or was he just throwing cards?

Too many finesses. The other declarer, instead of hoping for an ideal lie of the cards, tried to play assuming a lie that put the contract at risk. He thought about the bidding. After drawing trumps, he led ace and a low diamond.

If East had the diamond king and the finesse win, then West had the club ace for his opening bid. Declarer could safely lead toward the K-Q of clubs. West had to take the diamond king or lose it.

Now declarer could discard two clubs on the Q-J of diamonds. He lost one heart, one diamond, and one club.

144

WHICH FINESSE, ONE OR BOTH? NEITHER

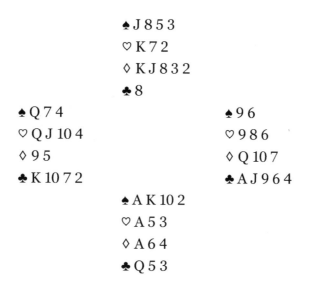

♠ J 8 5 3
♥ K 7 2
♦ K J 8 3 2
♣ 8

♠ Q 7 4
♥ Q J 10 4
♦ 9 5
♣ K 10 7 2

♠ 9 6
♥ 9 8 6
♦ Q 10 7
♣ A J 9 6 4

♠ A K 10 2
♥ A 5 3
♦ A 6 4
♣ Q 5 3

Contract: 4 ♠

Opening Lead: ♥ Queen

Declarer won the opening lead in dummy and took a trump finesse to the ten. West won and led another heart. Declarer won, drew trumps and took a diamond finesse. East won and returned another heart.

Declarer still had a club loser, down one. "Both finesses lost," moaned declarer, as North tried not to cry.

Question: How would you have handled these finesses?

At the other table, declarer realized this was a timing issue. He had to stay one step ahead, to dispose of his heart loser before it was too late.

Which finesse did he take? He took NO finesses.

After winning the opening lead in hand, saving the king, he played the A-K of trumps, then the A-K of diamonds and a third diamond. West discarded.

Now declarer had the heart king as an entry to the good diamonds, and could throw away his heart loser. He lost one trump, one diamond, and one club.

NO FINESSES, TOO MANY HCP'S

```
                    ♠ A Q 5
                    ♡ Q 7 3
                    ◇ K 8
                    ♣ Q J 10 7 5
    ♠ 10 9 8 7                      ♠ K J 4 2
    ♡ A                             ♡ 9 5 2
    ◇ 6 5 3 2                       ◇ Q 10 9 7 4
    ♣ K 9 8 3                       ♣ 2
                    ♠ 6 3
                    ♡ K J 10 8 6 4
                    ◇ A J
                    ♣ A 6 4
```

Contract: 4 ♡

Opening Lead: ♠ 10

Declarer, thinking the lead might have been from K 10 9 x, played the spade queen at trick one. East won the king and returned his singleton club. Declarer suddenly woke up, saw what was coming, and played the club ace.

He tried the heart ten, hoping to sneak a round of trumps thru. West won the ace, cashed the club king, and gave East a club ruff. Down one.

Question: What does too many HCP'S refer to? How should declarer play?

At the other table, declarer counted her tricks. She had one spade, five hearts, two diamonds, and four or five clubs. But she saw there may be four losers; one spade, one heart, and one club and a ruff.

Taking the ace of spades at trick one and drawing trumps as fast as possible would all but guarantee the contract.

Too many HCP's? Well, if the spade queen had been the deuce, declarer could not have gone wrong. Evil temptations, those 'mirage' queens.

LOTS OF FINESSES BUT WHAT'S THE HURRY?

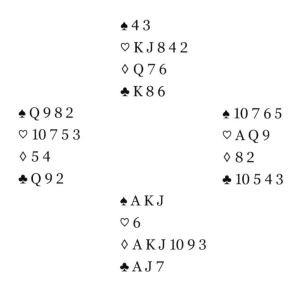

♠ 4 3
♡ K J 8 4 2
◇ Q 7 6
♣ K 8 6

♠ Q 9 8 2
♡ 10 7 5 3
◇ 5 4
♣ Q 9 2

♠ 10 7 6 5
♡ A Q 9
◇ 8 2
♣ 10 5 4 3

♠ A K J
♡ 6
◇ A K J 10 9 3
♣ A J 7

Contract: 6 ◇

Opening Lead: ◇ 4

Finesses everywhere. Declarer started by leading his heart. If he won a heart trick, the hand was over. If it lost, he wasn't down yet. West played low, declarer played the jack, East won the queen and returned a trump.

Declarer considered his options. He could take a spade finesse to discard a club, or try a club finesse. Another option was to cash the A-K of spades to try to drop the queen, then try the club finesse. All these options failed. Down one.

Question: Any thoughts? Any other options?

At the other table, declarer was in no hurry to try these finesses. He won the trump return in dummy and ruffed a heart. The ace was still missing. He cashed the A-K of spades and ruffed a spade.

When he ruffed another heart, finally the ace came crashing down. No finesses needed, thank you. He had a discard for his club loser. Had the ace not come down, then all right already, try a finesse, the LAST RESORT.

NO FINESSES: PREVENTING A RUFF

```
                        ♠ K 3
                        ♡ A Q J 10 6 4
                        ◊ K J 10 5
                        ♣ 4
        ♠ 10 6 2                        ♠ A 9 5 4
        ♡ 9 5 2                         ♡ K
        ◊ 2                             ◊ 9 8 6 3
        ♣ J 9 8 7 5 2                   ♣ Q 10 6 3
                        ♠ Q J 8 7
                        ♡ 8 7 3
                        ◊ A Q 7 4
                        ♣ A K
```

South	West	North	East	
1 NT	P	4 ◊*	P	* Texas transfer to hearts
4 ♡	P	4 NT ^	P	^ Key Card Blackwood
5 ♡		All Pass		

Opening Lead: ◊ 2

Declarer won in hand and led a heart to the queen. East won and returned a high diamond. West ruffed and returned a spade. Another diamond ruff meant down two.

"Did you think we were in six hearts?" asked North.

Question: What did North mean by his question?

At the other table, in the same contract with the same lead, declarer realized he could afford to lose one spade and one heart. He was not in six hearts, only five.

So he played a heart to the ace and made six.

RUFFING IN DECLARER'S HAND FOR TEN TRICKS

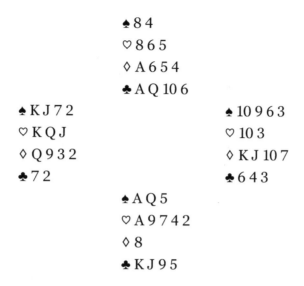

```
                      ♠ 8 4
                      ♡ 8 6 5
                      ◇ A 6 5 4
                      ♣ A Q 10 6
        ♠ K J 7 2                    ♠ 10 9 6 3
        ♡ K Q J                      ♡ 10 3
        ◇ Q 9 3 2                    ◇ K J 10 7
        ♣ 7 2                        ♣ 6 4 3
                      ♠ A Q 5
                      ♡ A 9 7 4 2
                      ◇ 8
                      ♣ K J 9 5
```

Contract: 4 ♡

Opening Lead: ♡ King

Declarer ducked the first trick and won the trump continuation. Looking to trump a spade in dummy, he took a spade finesse. West won and played the trump jack. No spade ruff.

West played a club and declarer only had nine tricks: four clubs, one diamond, one spade, and three trump tricks in hand. Down one.

Question: Was there a different road to ten tricks?

At the other table, declarer thought about the spade finesse. If it won, he was OK, but if it lost he had problems. So perhaps there was some other way home.

After winning the second heart, he started ruffing diamonds in his hand. He was able to ruff three diamonds regardless of who had the spade king.

He made four trump tricks in hand, plus four clubs and two outside aces.

That's ten, score it up.

NO FINESSES: ASSURE THE CONTRACT

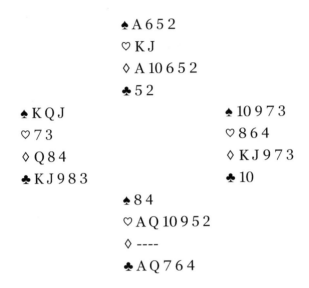

♠ A 6 5 2
♡ K J
◊ A 10 6 5 2
♣ 5 2

♠ K Q J
♡ 7 3
◊ Q 8 4
♣ K J 9 8 3

♠ 10 9 7 3
♡ 8 6 4
◊ K J 9 7 3
♣ 10

♠ 8 4
♡ A Q 10 9 5 2
◊ ----
♣ A Q 7 6 4

Contract: 4 ♡

Opening Lead: ♠ King

Declarer won the opening lead. He could count nine top tricks: six trump tricks in hand and three aces. There were two other possible tricks, a club finesse or a club ruff. He discarded his remaining spade on the diamond ace and tried Plan A, a club finesse.

West won and returned a trump. OK, Plan B. Declarer led a club, but East ruffed and returned a trump. There was no Plan C. Down one.

Question: Which "Plan" did you choose?

The declarer at the other table wanted to avoid any unnecessary finesses that might lead to trouble. Having avoided a trump opening lead, he could not be prevented from ruffing a club by just playing a club to the ace and conceding one club.

I wish I had a nickel for every queen 'mirage' in this book. One trump return now was fine. He could still ruff a club for his tenth trick.

FINESSE OR NOT: EIGHT EVER, NINE NEVER?

```
                    ♠ J 3
                    ♡ 9 7 6
                    ◊ Q J
                    ♣ K J 10 9 6 3
   ♠ 10 7 6 2                        ♠ 9 8 5 4
   ♡ 10 3                            ♡ J 8 5 2
   ◊ 10 6 5 ?                        ◊ A K 9 ?
   ♣ ? ?                             ♣ ? ?
                    ♠ A K Q
                    ♡ A K Q 4
                    ◊ 8 4 2
                    ♣ A 8 4
```

South	North
2 NT	3 NT
	All Pass

Opening Lead: ♠ 2

Declarer had eight top tricks. He needed a 3-3 split in hearts or a successful guess in clubs. South tried the hearts first. West discarded on the third heart.

Declarer now misguessed the club suit. Down one.

Question: Were there any clues to guide declarer to success?

At the other table, play started the same. When West showed out on the third heart, declarer tried to figure West's distribution. Probably four spades from the lead and known to have only two hearts.

If West had five diamonds, the opening lead might have been a diamond. So West rated to be either 4-2-4-3 or 4-2-3-4. This declarer played the ace of clubs, then took a successful club finesse.

151

FINESSE OR A BETTER PERCENTAGE PLAY?

```
                        ♠ A 8 3
                        ♡ A 9 6
                        ◊ A 5 4 2
                        ♣ 6 5 3
        ♠ Q 10 7                      ♠ J 9 5 4
        ♡ J 3 2                       ♡ Q 10 7 4
        ◊ J 10 9 8 7                  ◊ 3
        ♣ x x                         ♣ x x x x
                        ♠ K 6 2
                        ♡ K 8 5
                        ◊ K Q 6
                        ♣ A Q 7 4
```

Contract: 3 NT

Opening Lead: ◊ Jack

Declarer started with eight top tricks. He had good chances in the minors to develop one more, especially in clubs. He won the diamond ace, and played a club to the queen. West won the king and continued diamonds.

Declarer ended with the same eight tricks he started with, down one.

Question: Was that the best line? The other declarer made 3 NT.

At the other table, declarer took a higher percentage play in clubs. Needing only two tricks in the suit, low to the queen is 50%.

The other declarer knew a much higher percentage play for two tricks. He started with the ace, then led low from his hand. If nothing had happened, he planned to go to dummy and lead towards his queen.

Then if both followed, the suit had broken 3-3 and he had a ninth trick. If East started with K x x x, the ♣ Q would be the ninth trick.

West's ♣'s K 10

East's ♣'s J 9 8 2

FINESSE? MAYBE ONCE, BUT ENOUGH IS ENOUGH

```
                          ♠ A K
                          ♡ Q J 10 9
                          ◇ 5 4 3 2
                          ♣ 8 6 4
        ♠ 10 9 7 6 4                      ♠ 5 2
        ♡ K 4 2                           ♡ 7 6 5
        ◇ 10 6                            ◇ J 9 8 7
        ♣ J 9 2                           ♣ Q 10 5 3
                          ♠ Q J 8 3
                          ♡ A 8 3
                          ◇ A K Q
                          ♣ A K 7
```

Contract: 6 NT
Opening Lead: ♠ 10

Declarer counted lots of tricks. Being in dummy, there seemed to be no reason not to take a heart finesse. The queen of hearts won the trick. "Missed a grand, partner," said South. North just cringed.

Declarer led the heart jack, East played low, declarer, probably thinking about thirteen tricks, finessed again. West won and played another spade.

Thirteen, now forget twelve. With the heart suit blocked, and no way back to the hearts, declarer finished down one.

Question: How would you have played 6 NT?

The other declarer received the same opening lead. He realized one finesse was probably safe, but then he played a heart to his ace and led a small heart. If the defense ducked, he could continue hearts from the dummy.

Twelve tricks, the high spade was still in dummy to reach the good hearts if needed. Greed is not a good trait in a bridge player

TAKE A LOSING FINESSE TO
SAFEGUARD YOUR CONTRACT

This was a theme Michael Lawrence showed me a few years ago. Go out of your way to lose a finesse to protect your contract. Let's look:

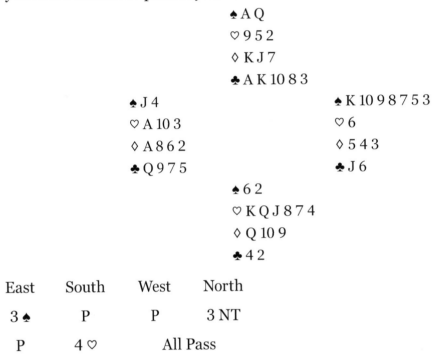

East	South	West	North
3 ♠	P	P	3 NT
P	4 ♡	All Pass	

Opening Lead: ♠ Jack

At the first table, declarer went up with the spade ace in a rush to draw trumps. Declarer led the heart jack, West won the ace and returned a spade. When East continued spades, the heart ten was promoted to the setting trick.

Question: How could you have prevented this?

The second declarer, having read a lot of Mike's great books, saw deeper into the hand. Sure, the finesse at trick one was going to lose. But if East had seven spades, taking the losing finesse would prevent West from getting a ruff, not having another spade to reach East when he later won the trump ace.

Sure, there were other dangers. East could have the club ace or a singleton somewhere, but this was the most obvious danger. By forcing East to win trick one there was no trump promotion.

COMBINING YOUR CHANCES

```
                    ♠ 7 2
                    ♡ 5 4
                    ◇ A Q 10 9 5 3
                    ♣ J 8 2
        ♠ K 10 8 4 3              ♠ J 9 5
        ♡ K 9 8 6 2              ♡ Q 10 7
        ◇ 4                       ◇ J 8 7 6
        ♣ K 5                     ♣ Q 7 4
                    ♠ A Q 6
                    ♡ A J 3
                    ◇ K 2
                    ♣ A 10 9 6 3
```

South	West	North	East
1 ♣	2 ♣	2 ◇	P
3 NT	All Pass		

Opening Lead: ♠ 4 (Unlucky guess)

Declarer won the opening lead and played the diamond king, then a small diamond. When West discarded, declarer tried a club. The defenders switched to hearts. Down one.

Question: How should declarer play to maximize his chances?

At the other table, declarer had listened to the bidding. To combine her chances, at trick two, she led the diamond two to the ten. If East won, she could overtake the king later and run the suit.

If East ducked, she could start the clubs, playing for split club honors. She could lead the club eight and let it ride. When in again, she could overtake the diamond king, cash the queen, and let the club jack ride, making an overtrick.

KEEP FINESSING LOW

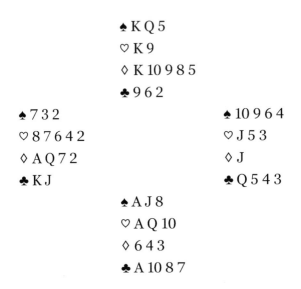

♠ K Q 5
♡ K 9
◇ K 10 9 8 5
♣ 9 6 2

♠ 7 3 2
♡ 8 7 6 4 2
◇ A Q 7 2
♣ K J

♠ 10 9 6 4
♡ J 5 3
◇ J
♣ Q 5 4 3

♠ A J 8
♡ A Q 10
◇ 6 4 3
♣ A 10 8 7

Contract: 3 NT
Opening Lead: ♡ 7

Declarer won the opening lead and came to hand to lead a diamond. West played low, declarer played the ten, losing to East's jack. East returned a heart. Declarer led another diamond. When West played low, declarer went up with the king.

The good news was it won, but East showed out. Declarer could only scramble eight tricks.

Question: How should declarer handle the diamonds?

The other declarer took a second diamond finesse, low to the nine, a far superior play. Playing the king only works where West started with A x x and East with Q J doubleton. Taking the second finesse was the right play.

NO FINESSE, ANOTHER MIRAGE

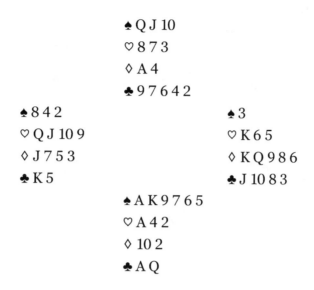

<pre>
                    ♠ Q J 10
                    ♡ 8 7 3
                    ◊ A 4
                    ♣ 9 7 6 4 2
        ♠ 8 4 2   ♠ 3
        ♡ Q J 10 9   ♡ K 6 5
        ◊ J 7 5 3   ◊ K Q 9 8 6
        ♣ K 5   ♣ J 10 8 3
                    ♠ A K 9 7 6 5
                    ♡ A 4 2
                    ◊ 10 2
                    ♣ A Q
</pre>

Contract: 4 ♠

Opening Lead: ♡ Queen

Declarer won the opening lead and played a spade to dummy. He led a club to his queen. West won, cashed two heart tricks, and led a diamond. Declarer won the ace, played a club to his ace and led another trump.

He ruffed a club but when West showed out, he still had a diamond loser. Down one.

Question: How would you have played to make four spades?

The other declarer saw the need to time the hand better. No finesse, thank you. The club queen was a 'mirage'. If it had been a deuce, as we have seen on many hands, how would you play?

He won the opening lead and played the A-Q of clubs. Now he had the timing to set up the clubs. The diamond loser was discarded on the fifth club.

DRAWING

TRUMPS

DRAWING TRUMPS: FINESSE?

$$\spadesuit\ K\ 6\ 4$$
$$\heartsuit\ A\ 8\ 6$$
$$\diamond\ K\ Q\ 6\ 4$$
$$\clubsuit\ 7\ 5\ 4$$

♠ Q J 10 9 2   ♠ A 7
♡ Q 5   ♡ 10 9 2
♢ 9 5   ♢ 8 7 3 2
♣ 8 6 3 2   ♣ Q J 10 9

♠ 8 5 3
♡ K J 7 4 3
♢ A J 10
♣ A K

Contract: 4 ♡

Opening Lead: ♠ Queen

Declarer ducked trick one, since he was sure East had the spade ace. West continued with the spade jack, declarer played low, and East played the ace. East returned the club queen.

Declarer won, played a heart to the ace and a heart to his jack. East and West each scored a trump trick. Down one.

Question: Is there a cure for this?

This is of course, an extreme example of: 1) I never met a finesse I didn't like, and 2) eight ever, nine never, I'm finessing, damn the torpedos.

My caddy knew East was waiting for a spade ruff.

At the other table, the declarer just cashed the A-K of trumps and was rewarded when the queen fell, making five hearts.

DRAWING TRUMPS: FINESSE?

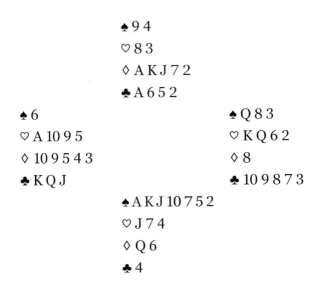

```
                        ♠ 9 4
                        ♡ 8 3
                        ◇ A K J 7 2
                        ♣ A 6 5 2
        ♠ 6                             ♠ Q 8 3
        ♡ A 10 9 5                      ♡ K Q 6 2
        ◇ 10 9 5 4 3                    ◇ 8
        ♣ K Q J                         ♣ 10 9 8 7 3
                        ♠ A K J 10 7 5 2
                        ♡ J 7 4
                        ◇ Q 6
                        ♣ 4
```

Contract: 4 ♠

Opening Lead: ♣ King

Another example of how to turn thirteen tricks into nine. Declarer won the opening lead and cashed the A-K of trumps. When West showed out on the second round, he tried to discard a heart on the diamonds.

East ruffed the second diamond. The defense cashed three heart tricks.

Question: Could you play this hand to assure your contract?

The other declarer also saw a possibility of thirteen tricks, but also saw the danger of a 3-1 spade split. He took a first round trump finesse. If it lost, the defense could only cash two heart tricks.

"Have to bid these slams, partner," said North.

DRAWING TRUMPS: FINESSE?

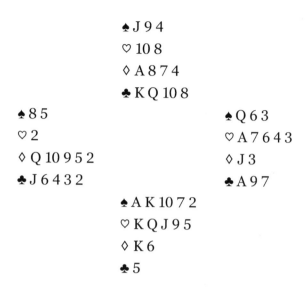

♠ J 9 4
♥ 10 8
♦ A 8 7 4
♣ K Q 10 8

♠ 8 5
♥ 2
♦ Q 10 9 5 2
♣ J 6 4 3 2

♠ Q 6 3
♥ A 7 6 4 3
♦ J 3
♣ A 9 7

♠ A K 10 7 2
♥ K Q J 9 5
♦ K 6
♣ 5

Contract: 4 ♠

Opening Lead: ♥ 2

East won the opening lead with the ace and cashed the ace of clubs. He then returned a heart, West ruffed with the five and returned a diamond. Declarer won and had to tackle the trump suit.

With four trumps remaining, he cashed the A-K, but West showed out on the second round. Down one.

"Are you paying any attention?" thought North.

Question: What was North thinking about? What inferences were available?

East defended well, but declarer should have been able to figure out the situation. At the other table, declarer asked himself why didn't East attempt to give West another heart ruff, trying for a trump promotion if West had ♠ Q x.

It could only be because East knew it would give away the location of the trump queen, when West couldn't ruff higher than the jack in dummy.

DRAWING TRUMPS: FINESSE?

```
                    ♠ Q 6 2
                    ♡ Q
                    ◊ K 7 6 5
                    ♣ K Q 9 6 4
    ♠ 9                           ♠ A J 8
    ♡ 10 9 7 4 3                  ♡ 8 6 2
    ◊ Q J 10 4 2                  ◊ A 9 8 3
    ♣ J 7                         ♣ A 10 3
                    ♠ K 10 7 5 4 3
                    ♡ A K J 5
                    ◊ ----
                    ♣ 8 5 2
```

Contract: 4 ♠

Opening Lead: ◊ Queen

South ruffed the opening lead and played a trump to the queen. East won and returned a trump. Declarer played the king, West discarded. Declarer cashed the heart queen, ruffed a diamond and led a club.

East won and cashed the high trump. Declarer still had to lose one more club. Down one.

Question: What ever happened to eight ever, nine never?

Again, it's a bridge hand. The other declarer took a trump finesse at trick three. If the finesse lost, she could discard three clubs from dummy on the high hearts, and there would still be a trump left in dummy for the last club.

A win-win situation.

DRAWING TRUMPS: FINESSE?

$\spadesuit$ A J 10 3 2
$\heartsuit$ A Q 5 4
$\diamond$ J 10 3
$\clubsuit$ A

$\spadesuit$ 7 $\spadesuit$ Q 8 5
$\heartsuit$ J 8 7 2 $\heartsuit$ 9 6
$\diamond$ K 8 5 4 2 $\diamond$ 9 7 6
$\clubsuit$ 10 9 3 $\clubsuit$ Q 7 6 4 2

$\spadesuit$ K 9 6 4
$\heartsuit$ K 10 3
$\diamond$ A Q
$\clubsuit$ K J 8 5

Contract: 6 $\spadesuit$

Opening Lead: $\clubsuit$ 10

Declarer won the opening lead. Lots of options in all the suits. "We might have missed a grand, partner," said South. North had heard this before, and thought to herself, "Please, just try to make six instead."

With nine trumps, declarer cashed the A-K, and West showed out on the second round. OK, no grand. Declarer tried to ruff out the club queen or drop the heart jack, but finally had to take the diamond finesse.

Down one. "Very nice," said North, "Six spades was cold."

Question: What line of play was North referring to?

Bridge is a bridge hand, not a suit. Declarer had nine trumps, but at the other table, after cashing the trump ace, he played the trump jack and let it ride.

If it lost, West would be endplayed in three suits. Declarer would get a free finesse for twelve tricks.

DRAWING TRUMPS: FINESSE?

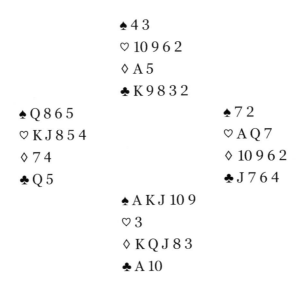

```
                        ♠ 4 3
                        ♡ 10 9 6 2
                        ◇ A 5
                        ♣ K 9 8 3 2
        ♠ Q 8 6 5                      ♠ 7 2
        ♡ K J 8 5 4                    ♡ A Q 7
        ◇ 7 4                          ◇ 10 9 6 2
        ♣ Q 5                          ♣ J 7 6 4
                        ♠ A K J 10 9
                        ♡ 3
                        ◇ K Q J 8 3
                        ♣ A 10
```

Contract: 4 ♠

Opening Lead: ♡ 5

Shortness in the long trump hand is usually a liability, not an asset. Declarer proved that by ruffing the second heart and going to dummy's ace of diamonds. He took a trump finesse. West won and returned another heart.

Declarer ruffed and cashed the A-K of trumps. When East discarded, declarer had only eight tricks. "Were you playing for overtricks?" asked North.

Question: How did the other declarer take ten tricks?

At the other table, declarer was concerned about losing control. After ruffing the second heart, he cashed the A-K of trumps. Then he started playing the good diamonds, being a step ahead in the tempo.

The defense could ruff once with the trump eight and continue hearts, but declarer was in control.

He lost one more trick to the trump queen. Making four spades.

FINESSE OR NOT: EIGHT EVER, NINE NEVER?

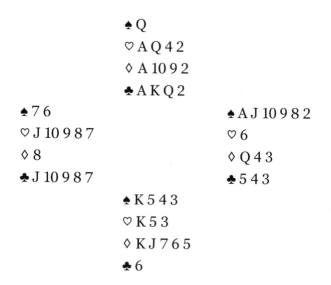

```
                    ♠ Q
                    ♡ A Q 4 2
                    ◊ A 10 9 2
                    ♣ A K Q 2
    ♠ 7 6                          ♠ A J 10 9 8 2
    ♡ J 10 9 8 7                   ♡ 6
    ◊ 8                            ◊ Q 4 3
    ♣ J 10 9 8 7                   ♣ 5 4 3
                    ♠ K 5 4 3
                    ♡ K 5 3
                    ◊ K J 7 6 5
                    ♣ 6
```

Contract: 6 ◊ (East opens 2 ♠)

Opening Lead: ♠ 7

East won the spade ace and returned the jack, West followed with the six. Declarer was only concerned about the trump queen; cash the A-K, or maybe play West for more length and take a finesse. He---went down one.

Question: How did the declarer at the other table make six diamonds?

The other declarer wasn't ready to make a decision at trick three. He played the heart king, both opponents followed, then a club to dummy and two more high clubs, discarding spades. He wasn't concerned if East ruffed but East followed.

Declarer led the spade ace, East discarded, and he discarded a heart. Declarer led and ruffed the last club from dummy, East showed out.

At this point declarer knows East started with exactly one spade, six hearts, and three clubs so three diamonds. Declarer cashed the diamond ace and took a finesse. Finding out the distribution is so often the key to playing a hand.

This theme is from a hand played in a tournament in the 1990's, and shown years ago in an issue of the "ACBL Bulletin".

FINESSE OR DROP: EIGHT EVER, NINE NEVER?

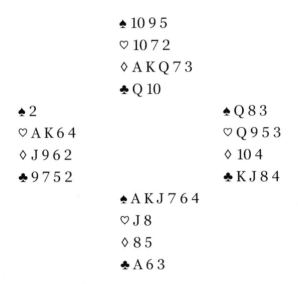

```
                          ♠ 10 9 5
                          ♡ 10 7 2
                          ◇ A K Q 7 3
                          ♣ Q 10
        ♠ 2                                   ♠ Q 8 3
        ♡ A K 6 4                             ♡ Q 9 5 3
        ◇ J 9 6 2                             ◇ 10 4
        ♣ 9 7 5 2                             ♣ K J 8 4
                          ♠ A K J 7 6 4
                          ♡ J 8
                          ◇ 8 5
                          ♣ A 6 3
```

Contract: 4 ♠

Opening Lead: ♡ Ace

Declarer ruffed the third round of hearts. With nine trumps, he cashed the A-K. Now declarer tried to set up the diamonds, but when they divided 4-2, he lacked entries back to dummy's last diamond.

Down one, losing two hearts, one spade, and one club.

Question: Unlucky or poorly planned? Too much attention to nursery rhymes?

Declarer should start the diamonds and take the trump finesse. If it loses, he can win the club return, but he has an extra entry in the trump suit to set up and use the diamonds.

The fact that the trump finesse wins is a bonus.

DRAWING TRUMPS: FINESSE?

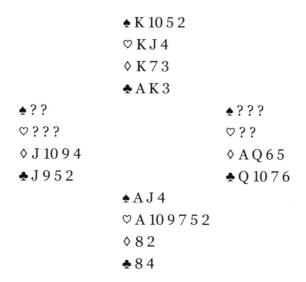

```
                    ♠ K 10 5 2
                    ♡ K J 4
                    ♢ K 7 3
                    ♣ A K 3
♠ ? ?                               ♠ ? ? ?
♡ ? ? ?                             ♡ ? ?
♢ J 10 9 4                          ♢ A Q 6 5
♣ J 9 5 2                           ♣ Q 10 7 6
                    ♠ A J 4
                    ♡ A 10 9 7 5 2
                    ♢ 8 2
                    ♣ 8 4
```

Contract: 4 ♡

Opening Lead: ♢ Jack

Declarer ruffed the third diamond and had potential losers in both majors. On a bad day, two more losers.

Declarer cashed the A-K of trumps and tried to guess the spades.

Question: I didn't tell you the result. Was this the correct play?

At the other table, the declarer saw a way to guarantee the contract. Do you see it? Before touching the majors, cash the A-K of clubs and ruff a club. Now cash the heart ace and play a heart to the jack.

Sure, you had nine trumps, but if East wins, he is endplayed. The minors have been eliminated. He must play a spade or give you a ruff/sluff.

DRAWING TRUMPS: EIGHT EVER, NINE NEVER; REALLY?

```
                    ♠ 5 4 2
                    ♡ K J 5 2
                    ◇ K 5 2
                    ♣ K 9 4
        ♠ 10 9 8 7              ♠ A K 6
        ♡ 8                     ♡ Q 9 6
        ◇ Q 10 8                ◇ 9 7 3
        ♣ Q 8 7 6 2             ♣ J 10 5 3
                    ♠ Q J 3
                    ♡ A 10 7 4 3
                    ◇ A J 6 4
                    ♣ A
```

Contract: 4 ♡

Opening Lead: ♠ 10

Declarer won the third spade. He cashed the A-K of trumps, West showed out. One discard on the club king didn't help. He took a diamond finesse. Down one.

Question: How would you handle the trump suit? Eight ever, nine never?

The other declarer was not a slave to nursery rhymes. This is a bridge hand, not an isolated suit. He first cashed the club ace, crossed to the heart king, discarded a diamond on the club king, and ruffed a club.

Only after the black suits were stripped was it time for the red suits. He led a heart from dummy. If East followed, declarer was playing the ten. West would be endplayed if he won.

Had East shown out, he would have played his ace and another trump, same result. No need to guess the diamond. Making four hearts either way.

DRAWING TRUMPS: FINESSE?

♠ ----
♡ K 7 3
◊ K J 8 7 5 2
♣ K Q 9 6

♠ 10 7 6 3
♡ A J 10 9 6 2
◊ A Q 3
♣ ----

Contract: 6 ♡
Opening Lead: ♠ Ace

Declarer ruffed the opening lead. Lots of tricks, but when he cashed the A-K of trumps, no queen. Now what? There was no road to twelve tricks. He could not get rid of those spades, no matter what.

Question: Could you have assured twelve tricks?

At the other table, declarer realized that as long as trumps were 2-2 or 3-1, the slam was coming home. He just had to get the queen of trumps out. At trick two he took a trump finesse, not caring if it won or lost.

He led a small trump from dummy and finessed.
1) If it won, he would play to the king of hearts, ruff a club and draw trumps.
2) If it lost, do the same thing, winning any return and draw trumps.

Anything would work, except cashing the A-K.

The E/W hands? Put the queen of trumps wherever you like.

DRAW TRUMPS: FINESSE?

                    ♠ A K
                    ♡ A 7 5 2
                    ◇ J 7 5
                    ♣ Q 10 6 4
    ♠ Q 9 6 5 2   ♠ J 8 7 3
    ♡ Q 10 8   ♡ 9 3
    ◇ A 10 2   ◇ K 9 8 6
    ♣ 8 3   ♣ 9 7 5
                    ♠ 10 4
                    ♡ K J 6 4
                    ◇ Q 4 3
                    ♣ A K J 2

Contract: 4 ♡

Opening Lead: ♠ 5

Declarer won the opening lead and cashed the heart ace. He then played a heart to the jack. West won the queen and played another spade. After drawing the last trump, declarer realized this hand was about diamonds.

He lost three diamond tricks, down one.

Question: Was four hearts cold with any 3-2 trump split?

At the other table, declarer looked at the whole hand, not just the trump suit. He cashed the A-K of trumps. If the queen had fallen, he could draw the last trump, but would likely lose three diamonds.

When the trump queen didn't fall, he just kept playing winners. When someone ruffed in, they would have to break the diamond suit, so he would only lose two diamonds. Or they would give him a ruff/sluff.

Four hearts was cold with or without a trump loser.

FROM THE TOP OR FINESSE

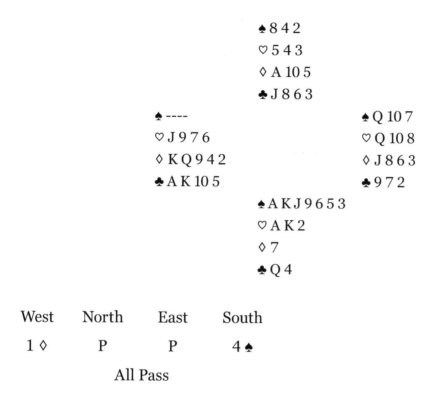

```
                    ♠ 8 4 2
                    ♡ 5 4 3
                    ◊ A 10 5
                    ♣ J 8 6 3
   ♠ ----                           ♠ Q 10 7
   ♡ J 9 7 6                        ♡ Q 10 8
   ◊ K Q 9 4 2                      ◊ J 8 6 3
   ♣ A K 10 5                       ♣ 9 7 2
                    ♠ A K J 9 6 5 3
                    ♡ A K 2
                    ◊ 7
                    ♣ Q 4
```

West	North	East	South
1 ◊	P	P	4 ♠
	All Pass		

Opening Lead: ♣ Ace

In the last round of a Swiss team match, West led the club ace, then switched to the diamond king. Declarer won the ace and played a spade to his ace. Down one.

Question: How did the declarer at the other table make four spades?

The other declarer did not have mirrors. But to assure his contract, he took a spade finesse. If it lost, he planned to force out the club king, then discard his heart loser on the club jack. The spade eight would be the entry.

If West had ♠ Q 10 7, there was nothing declarer could do. But he could protect against East having that holding. If spades were 2-1, nothing mattered.

Playing matchpoints, it's a whole different discussion. It's probably (?) right to cash the ♠ A-K.

DRAWING TRUMPS: MUST YOU FINESSE?

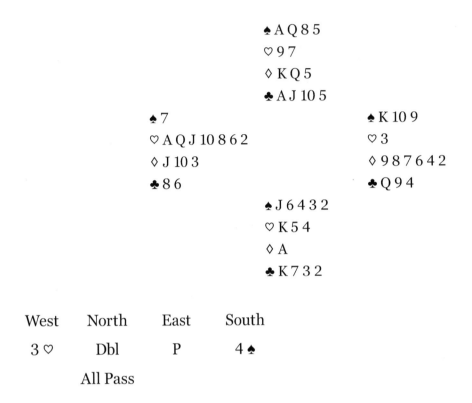

```
                        ♠ A Q 8 5
                        ♡ 9 7
                        ◊ K Q 5
                        ♣ A J 10 5
        ♠ 7                             ♠ K 10 9
        ♡ A Q J 10 8 6 2               ♡ 3
        ◊ J 10 3                       ◊ 9 8 7 6 4 2
        ♣ 8 6                          ♣ Q 9 4
                        ♠ J 6 4 3 2
                        ♡ K 5 4
                        ◊ A
                        ♣ K 7 3 2
```

West	North	East	South
3 ♡	Dbl	P	4 ♠
	All Pass		

Opening Lead: ◊ Jack

Declarer won the opening lead and led a spade to the queen. East won and returned a heart. West won two heart tricks and played a third heart.

East's ♠ 10 – 9 meant down one, no matter what South did.

Question: Is there a rule that you have to take every finesse you see?

At the other table, declarer doubted the spade finesse was going to succeed. To avoid this trump promotion, she led a spade to the ace. She then led a low spade from dummy. East had no answer.

East won the king and the defense took two heart tricks. But declarer had a high spade in dummy if West continued hearts. And there was no need to guess the clubs. Declarer discarded two clubs on the K-Q of diamonds in dummy.

ONE FINESSE IS ENOUGH

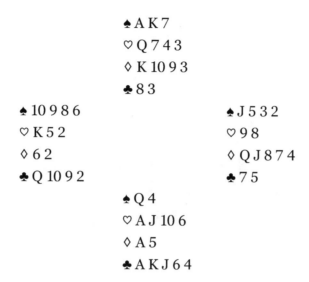

```
                ♠ A K 7
                ♡ Q 7 4 3
                ◊ K 10 9 3
                ♣ 8 3
  ♠ 10 9 8 6                    ♠ J 5 3 2
  ♡ K 5 2                       ♡ 9 8
  ◊ 6 2                         ◊ Q J 8 7 4
  ♣ Q 10 9 2                    ♣ 7 5
                ♠ Q 4
                ♡ A J 10 6
                ◊ A 5
                ♣ A K J 6 4
```

Contract: 6 ♡

Opening Lead: ♠ 10

Declarer won the opening lead in dummy to lead a trump to his ten. The ten won the trick as West played low smoothly. Declarer led a diamond to the king in dummy and returned a trump to his jack. West won the king and returned his last trump.

Now (finally) declarer counted his tricks. He played the A-K of clubs and ruffed a club, but when the suit divided 4-2, had a club loser at the end. Down one.

"Were you trying to make seven spades?" moaned North.

Question: What was North referring to? How would you have played?

Declarer could afford to lose one trump trick. After the first finesse won, the other declarer cashed the trump ace and went about his business, cashing winners and ruffing losers. He had sufficient trumps to ruff two clubs.

The defense won one trick at the end, the trump king.

173

NO
FINESSES
BASED
ON
HCP'S

NO FINESSE: COUNT THE HCP'S

```
                    ♠ J 10 7 6
                    ♡ 5 2
                    ◊ A Q J 9
                    ♣ K 8 2
        ♠ 8 3                         ♠ A 2
        ♡ K Q 4 3                     ♡ A 10 9 8 7
        ◊ 8 7 6 3 2                   ◊ K
        ♣ 7 5                         ♣ J 9 6 4 3
                    ♠ K Q 9 5 4
                    ♡ J 6
                    ◊ 10 5 4
                    ♣ A Q 10
```

East	South	West	North
1 ♡	1 ♠	2 ♡	3 ♡
P	4 ♠	All Pass	

Opening Lead: ♡ King

West led the heart king. East made a good play by overtaking with his ace, and switching to his singleton king of diamonds. A good play, easy with a singleton deuce, but more difficult with the king into the ◊ A Q J.

When East won the first trump trick, he led to West's queen of hearts. The diamond ruff was the setting trick. Well done!

Question: Without this great defense, how would declarer see the hand?

At the other table, West's heart king won and West continued with the heart queen. At trick three, he switched to a diamond. Declarer considered finessing, but counted the HCP's. East had opened the bidding and West had the ♡ K Q.

This finesse was not likely to succeed, so against the odds he played the ace and was rewarded.

It's never good to open the bidding and end up defending. Players open lighter and lighter these days, but give away a lot of information.

NO FINESSE: COUNT THE HCP'S

```
                    ♠ A J 7 3
                    ♡ J 9 7
                    ◇ A K 8 6 4
                    ♣ 4
        ♠ 8                         ♠ K 5
        ♡ K Q 10 3 2                ♡ A 6 5 4
        ◇ 5                         ◇ Q 10 7 3
        ♣ 10 9 8 7 3 2             ♣ Q J 6
                    ♠ Q 10 9 6 4 2
                    ♡ 8
                    ◇ J 9 2
                    ♣ A K 5
```

East	South	West	North
1 ◇	1 ♠	Dbl	2 ◇
2 ♡	3 ♠	4 ♡	4 ♠
P	P	5 ♡	5 ♠
	All Pass		

Opening Lead: ♡ King

A competitive auction. Declarer ruffed the second heart and took a spade finesse. East won and returned a spade. Declarer still had to lose a diamond. Down one.

Question: How did declarer in the other room make five spades?

Simple arithmetic. E/W have seventeen HCP's. If West has the K Q of hearts, my waiter knows who has the rest. So no spade finesse.

The other declarer played the spade ace. When the king of spades didn't fall, he played the A-K of clubs, discarding the last heart, and ruffed a club.

With the clubs and hearts eliminated, he played a trump. East had to lead away from his diamond queen or give declarer a ruff/sluff.

NO FINESSE: HCP'S AND OPENING LEAD

```
                    ♠ 7 5 2
                    ♡ K 9 4
                    ◊ J 7 4 3
                    ♣ K 7 5
   ♠ A Q 10 6 4                    ♠ K 9
   ♡ Q 3                           ♡ 10 8 6
   ◊ A 10                          ◊ 9 8 6 5
   ♣ J 10 9 4                      ♣ Q 8 6 3
                    ♠ J 8 3
                    ♡ A J 7 5 2
                    ◊ K Q 2
                    ♣ A 2
```

West	North	East	South	
1 ♠	P	1 NT*	2 ♡	* 1 round force
P	3 ♡	All Pass		

Opening Lead: ♣ Jack

Declarer won the club king, cashed the king of trumps, and played a trump to the jack. He lost three spade tricks, a diamond, and one trump. Down one. North was not happy.

Question: What was North muttering about? How should South play?

All the clues were there to avoid the trump finesse. Who has what, asked the other declarer? The opening lead gave away the whole show. East probably had the spade king, no spade lead (from A K or K Q), and East has the club queen.

Not much left for West's opening bid. The other declarer played the A-K of trumps, dropping the queen. Known from the opening lead to have five HCP's, the certainty of the trump queen being with West was almost 100%.

It's important to try to bid something. 1 NT, "forcing," doesn't promise anything, but on the other hand doesn't give everything away either.

NO FINESSE: COUNT THE HCP'S

                    ♠ Q 10 3
                    ♡ A Q 7 6
                    ◊ 7 4 2
                    ♣ J 7 5

    ♠ 7   ♠ 9 6 4
    ♡ J 9 8 3   ♡ K 10 4
    ◊ 10 8 6 5 3   ◊ K Q 9
    ♣ 10 9 2   ♣ K Q 8 4

                    ♠ A K J 8 5 2
                    ♡ 5 2
                    ◊ A J
                    ♣ A 6 3

East	South	West	North
1 ♣	1 ♠	P	2 ♠
P	4 ♠	All Pass	

Opening Lead: ♣ 10

Declarer won the opening lead and drew trumps. Faced with four possible losers, he took a heart finesse that rated to lose. No surprise there. Down one.

North said his partner must have been away during the bidding.

Question: Overbid, or was there a chance to make this?

At the other table, declarer saw a reasonable way home. The heart finesse offered almost no chance, but there was a better line. He won the opening lead and cashed the spade ace. He played a heart to dummy and played low. East won, cashed two club tricks, and played the king of diamonds.

Declarer won his ace, cashed the trump king, and played a heart to the ace. He led a low heart, down came the king from East and declarer ruffed.

A trump to dummy's queen drew the last trump. The heart queen was there to discard the diamond loser.

TWO POSSIBLE FINESSES BUT COUNT THE HCP'S

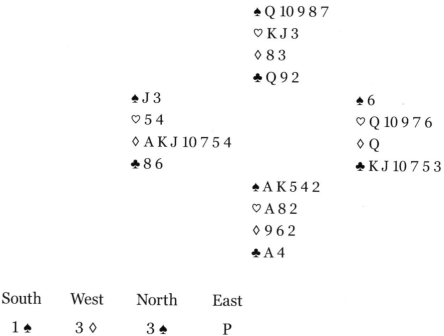

```
                          ♠ Q 10 9 8 7
                          ♡ K J 3
                          ◊ 8 3
                          ♣ Q 9 2
        ♠ J 3                              ♠ 6
        ♡ 5 4                              ♡ Q 10 9 7 6
        ◊ A K J 10 7 5 4                   ◊ Q
        ♣ 8 6                              ♣ K J 10 7 5 3
                          ♠ A K 5 4 2
                          ♡ A 8 2
                          ◊ 9 6 2
                          ♣ A 4
```

South	West	North	East
1 ♠	3 ◊	3 ♠	P
4 ♠	All Pass		

Opening Lead: ◊ Ace

Declarer lost the first two diamond tricks. There were still possible losers in hearts and clubs. Declarer ruffed the third diamond, drew trumps and tried first the club, then the heart finesses, down one.

Question: Were there any clues to the right line of play?

The other declarer drew trumps and thought more about the bidding. West preempted with ◊ A K J 10 x x x and the spade jack. If he had the club king, he probably would have bid 2 ◊, not 3 ◊. And there was the same inference with the heart queen.

So the other declarer cashed the A-K of hearts and exited a heart. East was endplayed.

NO FINESSE: TRY FOR A SINGLETON KING

♠ J 7
♡ 5 4 3
◇ A K Q 8
♣ J 7 4 3

♠ A Q 8 6 5   ♠ K 3
♡ Q J 7 2   ♡ 10 9 8 6
◇ J 9 6   ◇ 4 2
♣ K   ♣ 9 8 6 5 2

♠ 10 9 4 2
♡ A K
◇ 10 7 5 3
♣ A Q 10

West	North	East	South
1 ♠	P	P	1 NT
P	2 NT	P	3 NT
	All Pass		

Opening Lead: ♠ 6

E/W took the top three spade tricks, and gave declarer his spade ten. Searching for a ninth trick, declarer took a club finesse, down one.

Question: How would you have found a ninth trick?

The other declarer knew taking the club finesse was hopeless. East passed one spade and he has already shown up with the spade king. Two kings? I don't think so. And that would give West a ten count for his opening bid.

Play the club ace; every once in a while, it's a good day.

East's pass didn't matter much on this hand. But passing opening bids, you might as well tear up your cards if you end up defending. Declarer knows where every card is. Try to make some noise, do something.

NO FINESSE: TRY FOR A SINGLETON KING

```
                        ♠ A 8 3
                        ♡ Q 4 3
                        ◇ K 9 8 7 5
                        ♣ Q 7
        ♠ 7 6 4 2                      ♠ K
        ♡ K 9 2                        ♡ A J 8 6 5
        ◇ 6                            ◇ 4 3 2
        ♣ 9 6 5 4 2                    ♣ A 10 8 3
                        ♠ Q J 10 9 5
                        ♡ 10 7
                        ◇ A Q J 10
                        ♣ K J
```

East	South	West	North
1 ♡	1 ♠	P	2 ♡
P	3 ◇	P	4 ♠
	All Pass		

Opening Lead: ♡ 2

Declarer played low, East played the jack. East returned a diamond. Declarer won and lost a spade finesse to East's king. East gave West a diamond ruff, won the club return and gave West a second ruff. East continued hearts. When the smoke cleared, down three.

Question: Could South have done better or did East make a good play?

At the other table, South had just bid four spades, not giving away as much information about his hand. East returned a low heart to West's king at trick two. West played a third heart, declarer ruffed.

But now consider what this declarer knew. Where is the spade king? It has to be with East. Can West have two kings and three hearts? No, for two reasons: He probably would have raised to two hearts, and that would give the opening bidder only nine HCP's.

So this declarer closed his eyes and played the ace of spades. Voila!

*** Notice how the first defender did well to try to hide the location of the high cards. A very important defensive principle.

FINESSE OR NOT? ARE YOU TRYING TO GO DOWN?

```
                    ♠ 5 4 2
                    ♡ 8 6 5
                    ◊ J 8 7
                    ♣ A K J 9
     ♠ A K Q 8 7                    ♠ 9 6 3
     ♡ K 9 2                        ♡ 10 4
     ◊ 10 4                         ◊ 6 5 3 2
     ♣ 10 5 3                       ♣ 8 7 6 2
                    ♠ J 10
                    ♡ A Q J 7 3
                    ◊ A K Q 9
                    ♣ Q 4
```

West	North	East	South
1 ♠	P	P	Dbl
P	2 ♣	P	2 ♡
P	3 ♡	P	4 ♡
	All Pass		

Opening Lead: ♠ Ace

Declarer ruffed the third round of spades. Always up for a good finesse, he went to dummy with a diamond and took a heart finesse. West won the king, (shocking!) and led another spade.

East ruffed with the heart ten. South overruffed, but now West had the ♡ 9 7 behind declarer's ♡ A 7 for a trump promotion. Down one.

Question: Do you think South was just taking a 'practice' finesse?

Declarer set himself up to go down. At the other table, the declarer was listening to the bidding, a good idea.

The heart king was with West or he would not have opened. So he started the trumps from the top, avoiding the trump promotion.

Some declarers just can't turn down a finesse.

DANGER

HANDS

WHICH FINESSE?

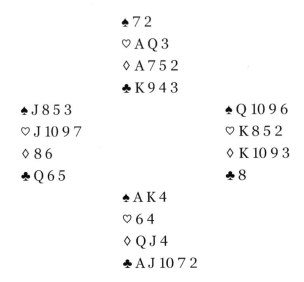

```
                    ♠ 7 2
                    ♡ A Q 3
                    ◊ A 7 5 2
                    ♣ K 9 4 3
   ♠ J 8 5 3                      ♠ Q 10 9 6
   ♡ J 10 9 7                     ♡ K 8 5 2
   ◊ 8 6                          ◊ K 10 9 3
   ♣ Q 6 5                        ♣ 8
                    ♠ A K 4
                    ♡ 6 4
                    ◊ Q J 4
                    ♣ A J 10 7 2
```

Contract: 3 NT
Opening Lead: ♡ Jack

Declarer at the first table saw lots of tricks and lots of finesses. He started with the heart finesse, playing the queen. East won and returned a heart. Declarer came to his hand with a spade and took a diamond finesse. East won and the defense cashed two heart tricks.

Declarer, tired of losing finesses, decided to trust the tried and true nursery rhyme 'eight ever, nine never', and cashed the A-K of clubs. Down one.

"I picked the wrong finesse," moaned South. North was looking around the room for a new partner for next week's duplicate.

Question: What kind of hand is this? Was declarer just unlucky?

Bridge is a hand, not just a suit. At the other table, declarer was in no hurry to try to win a trick with the queen at trick one. This is a 'danger' hand. If he could keep East on lead, the heart suit was safe.

So he took the heart ace and played a club to the ace. He led the club jack and let it ride. If the finesse lost, East could not play another heart. When the jack won, he safely took a diamond finesse. He finished with an overtrick.

TAKE AN UNNECESSARY FINESSE
WHEN DANGER LURKS

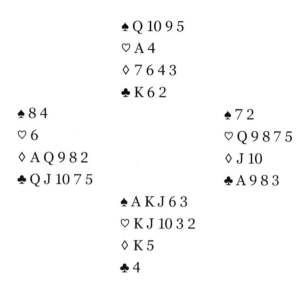

```
                    ♠ Q 10 9 5
                    ♡ A 4
                    ◊ 7 6 4 3
                    ♣ K 6 2
        ♠ 8 4                          ♠ 7 2
        ♡ 6                            ♡ Q 9 8 7 5
        ◊ A Q 9 8 2                    ◊ J 10
        ♣ Q J 10 7 5                   ♣ A 9 8 3
                    ♠ A K J 6 3
                    ♡ K J 10 3 2
                    ◊ K 5
                    ♣ 4
```

Contract: 4 ♠

Opening Lead: ♣ Queen

Declarer ruffed the second club and drew trumps. He cashed the A-K of hearts, West showed out. Declarer could ruff two hearts in dummy, but East was going to win the fifth heart. East now led the diamond jack. Down one.

Question: What kind of hand was this? What finesse was there to avoid?

If you recognize the hand pattern, you can see it's a danger hand. Declarer had to keep East off lead. So after drawing trumps, the other declarer played a heart to dummy's ace, then a heart to his jack, an unnecessary, but necessary finesse.

If it lost, West could not attack declarer's diamond position. If West won the queen of hearts and returned a club, declarer would ruff, and discard three diamonds from dummy on his ♡ K 10 3.

Making four spades, losing one heart, one club and one diamond if the finesse lost, or one club and two diamonds if it won.

DANGER HAND: AN UNNECESSARY FINESSE

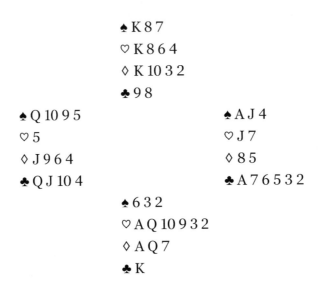

Contract: 4 ♡

Opening Lead: ♣ Queen

Declarer ruffed the second club and drew trumps. He played three rounds of diamonds needing a 3-3 split, the jack dropping, or East to have the fourth diamond. In the last situation, declarer could play the last diamond, discarding a spade, a loser-on-loser play. East would have been endplayed.

Unfortunately, none of the three scenarios came true. West had four diamonds. Declarer had to play the spades himself. Down one.

Question: Unlucky? Every card was wrong, but so was declarer's play.

The other declarer recognized this as a danger hand. After drawing trumps, he cashed the A-Q of diamonds and led a diamond. When West followed, he played the ten from dummy, not caring if it won or lost.

If it won, he had a good diamond to discard a spade. If it lost, East could not attack spades and declarer would have the diamond king to discard a spade.

DANGER HAND: IF YOU MUST FINESSE, IN WHAT ORDER?

```
                    ♠ A 9 4 3
                    ♡ 10 6 2
                    ◊ A 10 9
                    ♣ Q 10 8
    ♠ Q J 10 8 2                    ♠ K 6 5
    ♡ K 7 5                         ♡ 8 4
    ◊ 5 2                           ◊ K 7 6 4 3
    ♣ K 6 5                         ♣ 7 3 2
                    ♠ 7
                    ♡ A Q J 9 3
                    ◊ Q J 8
                    ♣ A J 9 4
```

South	West	North	East
1 ♡	1 ♠	1 NT	P
2 ♣	P	3 ♡	P
4 ♡	All Pass		

Opening Lead: ♠ Queen

Declarer was faced with lots of finesses, but no options. He won the ace of spades and took a trump finesse. West won and returned a spade. Declarer ruffed, drew trumps, and took a diamond finesse. East won and returned a spade.

Declare ruffed with his last trump. He went to dummy and took a club finesse. West won and cashed two spades, down two.

"Zero for three," lamented South. North was still looking, even harder.

Question: Unlucky yes, but could you have timed this differently?

At the other table, declarer saw this correctly as a danger hand. What could go wrong, that old question. Playing on the assumption that all the finesses were going to lose, declarer wanted to lose the last one to East. Why?

Because likely by then yes, declarer would be out of trumps, but East would be out of spades. His order of finesses was hearts (trumps), clubs, and finally diamonds. Making four hearts.

DANGER HAND: A DEEP FINESSE

                                    ♠ K 10 8 7
                                    ♡ A
                                    ◇ 6 3 2
                                    ♣ K 9 8 7 3
          ♠ 3   ♠ 9
          ♡ K Q J 9 6 2   ♡ 8 7 5 4 3
          ◇ K J 10 9   ◇ 8 7 5 4
          ♣ 6 4   ♣ A J 5
                                    ♠ A Q J 6 5 4 2
                                    ♡ 10
                                    ◇ A Q
                                    ♣ Q 10 2

South	West	North	East
1 ♠	2 ♡	3 ♡	4 ♡
4 ♠	5 ♡	P	P
5 ♠		All Pass	

Opening Lead: ♡ King

Declarer won the opening lead and drew trumps. He led a club from the board to
his queen, which won. He then played a club to the nine and East's jack. East returned
a diamond. Down one.

Question: Do you see a line of play to guarantee your contract?

At the other table, declarer recognized the danger of East playing a diamond before
the clubs were set up. After drawing trumps, he played the first club from dummy,
East had to play low. Declarer played his ten.

If West won with the jack, he could not attack diamonds. If he won with the ace,
the clubs were good. If the ten won, declarer could continue clubs to set up a trick for
a diamond discard, losing only one club.

WIN OR FINESSE? DANGER HAND

```
                    ♠ 6 2
                    ♡ A 5
                    ◊ J 10 9 6 4
                    ♣ Q J 7 6
        ♠ K J 10 8 5              ♠ 9 7 4 3
        ♡ 7 4 2                   ♡ K J 10 9 3
        ◊ K 5                     ◊ 3 2
        ♣ 10 8 3                  ♣ 9 5
                    ♠ A Q
                    ♡ Q 8 6
                    ◊ A Q 8 7
                    ♣ A K 4 2
```

South	West	North	East
2 NT	P	3 NT	All Pass

Opening Lead: ♡ 7

Declarer, thinking the lead was likely fourth best, played low, expecting to probably win with his queen. But East won and shifted to a spade. This finesse lost and another spade came back.

When the diamond finesse lost (sounds like a broken record, lost, lost, lost), declarer finished down two. When comparing with his teammates, his counterpart asked, "How many overtricks did you make?" Painful.

Question: How did the other declarer take make so many tricks?

The is a classic danger hand situation. The necessary diamond finesse, if it lost, would put West on lead. But by winning the first heart, declarer would have the guarded ♡ Q 8 and the ♠ A Q and lots of tricks.

Don't finesse out of habit. Consider the whole hand, not just a suit.

WIN, FINESSE, OR WHAT?

```
                        ♠ Q 6 5
                        ♡ A Q 4
                        ◊ K Q 9 5
                        ♣ 6 3 2
        ♠ J 9 4 3                        ♠ 10
        ♡ J 7 5 3                        ♡ K 10 8
        ◊ A 6 2                          ◊ 8 7 4 3
        ♣ 10 7                           ♣ Q J 8 5 4
                        ♠ A K 8 7 2
                        ♡ 9 6 2
                        ◊ J 10
                        ♣ A K 9
```

Contract: 4 ♠

Opening Lead: 3 ♡

Declarer saw no reason not to finesse the queen of hearts. East won and returned a heart. Declarer won and started drawing trumps. West had a trump trick. When declarer started diamonds, West won the second diamond, cashed a heart trick and played a club. Down one.

Question: It looks like four losers. Was there a better line of play?

At the other table, realized that yes, if everything was rosy, he might take twelve tricks. But by ducking altogether, neither winning nor finessing, there was a safer line. He played low.

East won but could not return the suit, so he switched to a club. Now declarer had the timing to draw trumps and start the diamonds. When East won the diamond ace, declarer still had the heart ace, and discarded losers on the long diamonds. He lost one spade, one heart, and one diamond. No finesses.

AVOIDANCE FINESSES: SPOT CARDS MEAN A LOT

```
                    ♠ K Q 5
                    ♡ A J 5 4
                    ◊ 7 2
                    ♣ A J 5 4
        ♠ 9 4                       ♠ 10 8 6 2
        ♡ 9 7 6 2                   ♡ Q 8 3
        ◊ A 10 8 5 4                ◊ Q 9 3
        ♣ 8 2                       ♣ K 7 6
                    ♠ A J 7 3
                    ♡ K 10
                    ◊ K J 6
                    ♣ Q 10 9 3
```

Contract: 3 NT
Opening Lead: ◊ 5

East played the queen, declarer won with the king and carelessly took a club finesse, perhaps mesmerized by the club spots. East won the king and returned the diamond nine. At least it was over quickly. Down one.

Question: Was there a safer road to 3 NT?

One suit may look good, but appearances can be deceiving. What kind of hand is this? Yes, a danger hand. Declarer cannot let East gain the lead.

There is another less mesmerizing but worthwhile finesse waiting. The heart ten, just begging to be noticed.

Even if a heart to the ten loses, West cannot attack your guarded ◊ J 6.

Declarer has one diamond, four spades, one club, and three or four hearts depending on the heart finesse.

WHICH FINESSE? NO FINESSE

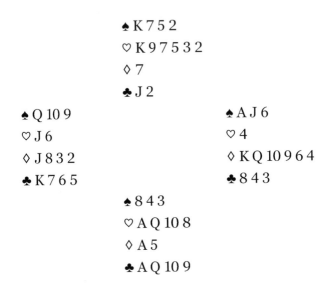

♠ K 7 5 2
♡ K 9 7 5 3 2
♢ 7
♣ J 2

♠ Q 10 9   ♠ A J 6
♡ J 6   ♡ 4
♢ J 8 3 2   ♢ K Q 10 9 6 4
♣ K 7 6 5   ♣ 8 4 3

♠ 8 4 3
♡ A Q 10 8
♢ A 5
♣ A Q 10 9

Contract: 4 ♡

Opening Lead: ♢ 2

Declarer won the opening lead. He had one potential club loser and three potential spade losers. He won the opening lead and drew trumps. He took the club finesse, hoping to discard dummy's spades. He lost the four tricks he feared. Down one.

Question: How did the declarer at the other table make four hearts?

What kind of hand is this? A danger hand. Declarer ducked the opening lead, a key play. East switched to a club. Declarer won the ace and drew trumps ending in his hand. He discarded dummy's remaining club on the diamond ace, and started playing clubs thru West, the danger hand. What could the defense do?

If West had the club king and covered, declarer could ruff and had two good clubs to discard two spades. If West didn't cover, declarer could keep leading clubs, discarding spades.

If East won the club king, the best he could do would be exit a club or cash a spade. Either way, declarer could not lose more than three tricks.

SQUEEZE
PLAY

FINESSE OR SQUEEZE?

```
                  ♠ J 3
                  ♡ K J 4 2
                  ◊ 7 5 2
                  ♣ A Q 4 2
        ♠ K 9 8 6              ♠ 10 7 5 2
        ♡ 6 5 3               ♡ 8
        ◊ 6 4                 ◊ A K J 9 8
        ♣ 10 9 8 6            ♣ J 7 5
                  ♠ A Q 4
                  ♡ A Q 10 9 7
                  ◊ Q 10 3
                  ♣ K 3
```

West	North	East	South
P	P	P	1 NT
P	2 ♣	2 ◊	2 ♡
P	4 ♡	All Pass	

Opening Lead: ◊ 6

East won the first two tricks and West ruffed the third round of diamonds. West returned the club ten. Declarer won, drew trumps and took a spade finesse. Down one.

Question: Was there any hope after losing the first three tricks?

East passed in third seat with ◊ A K J 9 8 and perhaps the club jack. The odds of a favorable spade finesse looked slim.

The other declarer decided to play for a squeeze. If West had four clubs, after cashing the trumps, West could not keep both four clubs and two spades.

West smoothly bared his spade king on the run of the trumps. But when no clubs were discarded, declarer cashed the spade ace, dropping the king.

194

FINESSE OR SQUEEZE

```
                    ♠ A Q J 3
                    ♡ Q 6 3
                    ◊ 10 8 4
                    ♣ 8 6 3
    ♠ K 10 7 5                      ♠ 8 6 2
    ♡ 4                             ♡ 9 8 5 2
    ◊ K 6 5 3 2                     ◊ 9 7
    ♣ K Q J                         ♣ A 10 7 2
                    ♠ 9 4
                    ♡ A K J 10 7
                    ◊ A Q J
                    ♣ 9 5 4
```

South	West	North	East
1 ♡	Dbl	Rdbl	P
P	1 ♠	2 ♡	P
4 ♡	All Pass		

Opening Lead: ♣ King

West cashed the K-Q of clubs, East overtook the third round with the ace, and shifted to a diamond. With a successful spade finesse providing only one discard, declarer took the diamond finesse without much hope. Down one.

Question: A pushy four heart contract, but was there any successful line?

The other declarer was not taking a losing finesse. He won the diamond ace, played two rounds of trumps, being careful to keep an entry to his hand. He finessed the spade. After two more rounds of trumps, nine tricks had been played. The position:

```
              ♠ A Q 3    ♡ ----     ◊10      ♣ ----
♠ K 10 7 ♡ ---- ◊ K ♣ ----
              ♠ 4        ♡ 7        ◊ Q J     ♣ ----
```

On the play of the last trump, West was squeezed. To keep three spades, he must discard the diamond king. To keep the diamond king, he must discard a spade.

195

FINESSE OR SQUEEZE

                        ♠ A J 9 8
                        ♡ A K J
                        ◊ Q 9 5
                        ♣ A Q J
        ♠ 5 4   ♠ 3
        ♡ 10 9 6 3   ♡ Q 7 5 4
        ◊ J 6   ◊ A K 8 3 2
        ♣ 9 8 5 3 2   ♣ K 7 4
                        ♠ K Q 10 7 6 2
                        ♡ 8 2
                        ◊ 10 7 4
                        ♣ 10 6

East	South	West	North
1 ◊	2 ♠	P	4 ♠
	All Pass		

Opening Lead: ◊ Jack

The defense started with A-K of diamonds, West ruffed the third diamond, and led the three of clubs. If either the heart or club finesse were successful, declarer would make four spades. He took the club finesse. Down one.

Question: Do you think either of the two finesses had any chance of success?

No. The other declarer said no losing finesses, thank you. She won the club ace, drew trumps, and cashed the heart ace. She returned to her hand and played the remaining trumps. The position with three tricks to be played:

            ♠ ---- ♡ K J ◊ --- ♣ Q   EAST
                                            ♠ ---- ♡ Q 7 ◊ ---- ♣ K
            ♠ 10 ♡ 8 ◊ --- ♣ 10

Declarer led her last trump, discarding the club queen. East was squeezed. Any discard gave declarer the rest of the tricks.

FINESSE OR SQUEEZE?

```
                    ♠ 10 7 3
                    ♡ Q 7 5 3
                    ◊ A K J 4
                    ♣ 9 7
        ♠ 4                         ♠ Q J 9 6 5
        ♡ 10 8 6 4 2               ♡ K 9
        ◊ 10 8 6                   ◊ Q 9 5 2
        ♣ 10 8 4 2                 ♣ J 3
                    ♠ A K 8 2
                    ♡ A J
                    ◊ 7 3
                    ♣ A K Q 6 5
```

Contract: 6 NT
Opening Lead: ♠ 4

Declarer won the opening lead and played the four rounds of clubs. West won and switched to the six of diamonds. Declarer won the ace and played a heart to his jack. He cashed the last club and the heart ace. Now, he took a diamond finesse. Down one.

Question: How did the other declarer make 6 NT?

The other declarer understood the pressure on the East hand. The early play was the same, but he did not take the diamond finesse. He played a diamond to the ace to reach this position. He cashed the heart queen.

```
        North  ♠ 7 ♡ Q ◊ J ♣ --
                                        East  ♠ Q J ♡ - ◊ Q ♣ --
        South  ♠ A 8 2 ♡ -- ◊ -- ♣ --
```

East was finished. If he threw the queen of diamonds, dummy's jack was high. If he threw a spade, declarer's spades were high.

FINESSE OR SQUEEZE? WATCH THE DISCARDS

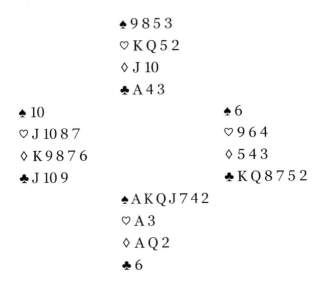

```
              ♠ 9 8 5 3
              ♡ K Q 5 2
              ◊ J 10
              ♣ A 4 3
♠ 10                        ♠ 6
♡ J 10 8 7                  ♡ 9 6 4
◊ K 9 8 7 6                 ◊ 5 4 3
♣ J 10 9                    ♣ K Q 8 7 5 2
              ♠ A K Q J 7 4 2
              ♡ A 3
              ◊ A Q 2
              ♣ 6
```

Contract: 7 ♠

Opening Lead: ♣ Jack

Declarer won the opening lead and drew the trumps. With not much to go on, he took a diamond finesse. Down one.

Question: How would you have played?

There was no rush to finesse. The other declarer starting by cashing all his trumps. On the second trump, West discarded the diamond nine. "Well, I believe you," thought declarer. He cashed the diamond ace and ran all his trumps.

West had to keep four hearts, so he threw away the diamond king, hoping East had the diamond queen. If West had just discarded low diamonds, and bared his king, declarer would have had to guess: squeeze or finesse?

It's not a good idea to signal declarer. At least don't tell the truth if you do.

TRYING TO AVOID BOTH FINESSES

♠ A 8
♡ K J 8 4
◊ 10 6 3
♣ Q J 8 4

♠ Q 7 4   ♠ 10 9 6 3 2
♡ 6 5   ♡ 7
◊ K Q J 9 7   ◊ 8 4 2
♣ K 9 7   ♣ 10 5 3 2

♠ K J 5
♡ A Q 10 9 3 2
◊ A 5
♣ A 6

Contract: 6 ♡ (West overcalls diamonds)
Opening Lead: ◊ King

Declarer had a good plan. Win the opening lead and draw trumps. He could take the spade finesse, discard dummy's diamond on the high spade and exit a diamond. With the diamonds and spades eliminated, West would be endplayed.

Good plan, but unfortunately West also had the spade queen. Down one.

Question: Can you come up with a different plan?

At the other table, the declarer considered the same plan but didn't want to rely on the spade finesse. After drawing trumps, he played the A-K of spades and ruffed a spade. Then he played all his trumps and kept count of the diamonds.

With three cards left: North: ◊ 10 ♣ Q J
 West: ◊ Q ♣ K 9 or ◊ Q J ♣ K

             South: ◊ 5 ♣ A 6

If West had two diamonds, South's clubs were good. If West had one diamond, South could exit a diamond and West was endplayed.

FINESSE OR SQUEEZE

```
                    ♠ K J 5 3
                    ♡ Q J
                    ◇ J 8 5 4 3
                    ♣ K 3
      ♠ 10 9 7 2                    ♠ Q 6 4
      ♡ 6 5 4 3 2                   ♡ A 10 8
      ◇ 9 7 6                       ◇ 2
      ♣ 5                           ♣ A Q 10 9 6 4
                    ♠ A 8
                    ♡ K 9 7
                    ◇ A K Q 10
                    ♣ J 8 7 2
```

East	South	West	North
1 ♣	1 NT	P	2 ♣
Dbl	2 ◇	P	3 NT
	All Pass		

Opening Lead: ♣ 5

East took the A-Q of clubs, West discarded a spade, and continued with the club ten. Declarer could count eight tricks. East was marked with the ace of hearts for his opening bid, and probably the spade queen. Declarer took a spade finesse. Down a few. "Did you have three spades," asked South.

North was muttering to himself about a new partner.

Question: Why was North muttering? How could you have made 3 NT?

The other declarer cashed five diamond tricks before making a decision. East followed once, then discarded two hearts, one club, and one spade.

Declarer knew East started with three hearts (he still had the presumed ace), one diamond, and six clubs, 3-3-1-6 distribution. He had only two spades left. Declarer cashed the A-K of spades and watch the queen fall. If East had discarded two clubs instead, it would have been safe to play a heart.

WHICH FINESSE? ANOTHER LINE OF PLAY?

```
                           ♠ A J 9
                           ♡ 6 5 4
                           ◇ A J 3
                           ♣ A K J 7
        ♠ 10 2                              ♠ 6 3
        ♡ A K J 10 9 3                      ♡ 2
        ◇ 10 8                              ◇ K 9 6 5 4 2
        ♣ 5 4 2                             ♣ Q 9 6 3
                           ♠ K Q 8 7 5 4
                           ♡ Q 8 7
                           ◇ Q 7
                           ♣ 10 8
```

West	North	East	South
2 ♡	Dbl	P	4 ♠
	All Pass		

Opening Lead: ♡ Ace

West led the A-K of hearts and gave East a heart ruff. East returned a spade. Declarer drew trumps. East likely had the diamond king from the bidding. Declarer took a club finesse trying to discard his diamond loser. Down one.

Question: Do you see any successful line of play? Yes, a Vienna Coup squeeze.

The other declarer wanted to save any finesse as a LAST RESORT. Cashing all the trumps would squeeze dummy in front of East. He drew two rounds of trumps and cashed the ace of diamonds to establish a threat card in his hand. Now he cashed more trumps., leaving this 4-card ending:

```
        ♠ ---- ♡ ---- ◇ J ♣ A K J            East
                                             ♠ --- ♡ -- ◇ K ♣ Q 9 6
        ♠ 4 ♡ --- ◇ Q ♣ 10 8
```

Declarer played the last trump, discarding the diamond jack. East was squeezed. South watched the discards. If the diamond king had not appeared, the clubs were good.

In hindsight, an opening club or diamond lead would have been better. Sure.

FINESSE? LATER, SQUEEZE FIRST

♠ 6 5 4
♡ J 9 6 2
◊ Q 4
♣ A Q J 3

♠ A K 9 8 7
♡ 4
◊ J 9 7
♣ K 7 5 2

♠ J 10
♡ 10 3
◊ K 8 5 3 2
♣ 10 9 6 4

♠ Q 3 2
♡ A K Q 8 7 5
◊ A 10 6
♣ 8

West	North	East	South
P	P	P	1 ♡
1 ♠	2 ♠	P	4 ♡
	All Pass		

Opening Lead: ♠ Ace

West led the A-K of spades and gave East a spade ruff. East returned a trump. Declarer drew trumps and took a club finesse, trying to ruff out the club king. Down one.

Question: Was there a successful line of play? Yes, a transfer squeeze.

The other declarer knew he needed West to have the club king. But as a passed hand, West could not also have the diamond king. To increase his chances for a squeeze, after the same first four tricks, declarer led the diamond queen, king, ace. Declarer cashed the last heart. West was squeezed.

North: ♠ -- ♡ -- ◊ -- ♣ A Q J 3

West: ♠ --- ♡ --- ◊ J ♣ K 7 5

South ♠ -- ♡ 5 ◊ 10 6 ♣ 8

West discarded a club to save the diamond jack. Now a club finesse, and then the king came down. Yes, a club return at trick four removes the entry.

SAVE THE FINESSE TILL THE END BUT THEN THINK

```
                    ♠ Q 8 4
                    ♡ K 8 7 6
                    ◊ 3 2
                    ♣ A K J 2
      ♠ J 10 9 7 6                    ♠ 3 2
      ♡ Q 2                           ♡ J 10 9 3
      ◊ X 4                           ◊ X 9 8 7 6
      ♣ 8 7 6 4                       ♣ 10 5
                    ♠ A K 5
                    ♡ A 5 4
                    ◊ A K J 5
                    ♣ Q 9 3
```

Contract: 6 NT
Opening Lead: ♠ Jack

Declarer saw eleven top tricks. An extra trick could come from a 3-3 heart split or a successful diamond finesse. To combine his chances, declarer played a low heart from each hand. He won the return and cashed the A-K of hearts. When hearts were 4-2, he took a diamond finesse.

Question: What was the result? What happened at the other table?

The other declarer started the same, but when hearts were 4-2, East having four, the finesse could wait. He cashed one high diamond, then his club and spade winners ending in the dummy. With two cards to go he led a diamond:

```
                ♠ - ♡ 6 ◊ 3 ♣ ----
   ♠ 10 ♡ - ◊ X ♣ --              ♠ - ♡ J ◊ X ♣ --
                ♠ - ♡ - ◊ K J ♣ ---
```

East played a low diamond, should you finesse? Well, East's last card is known to be the last heart so West must have the diamond queen. Play for the drop. This is called a show-up squeeze, no finesse please.

NO FINESSE NEEDED: SHOW - UP SQUEEZE

```
                    ♠ J 10 7
                    ♡ Q 8 3
                    ◇ K 8 6 2
                    ♣ K 8 5
        ♠ K 5 2                   ♠ 4 3
        ♡ A K J 5 4 2             ♡ 10 7
        ◇ 4 3                     ◇ J 10 9 5
        ♣ Q 6                     ♣ 10 9 4 3 2
                    ♠ A Q 9 8 6
                    ♡ 9 6
                    ◇ A Q 7
                    ♣ A J 7
```

South	West	North	East
1 ♠	2 ♡	2 ♠	P
4 ♠		All Pass	

Opening Lead: ♡ Ace

West led the A-K-J of hearts. East ruffed the third heart and declarer overruffed. He went to dummy's club king and took a trump finesse. West won and returned a trump. Declarer drew the last trump and started the diamonds, hoping for a 3-3 split. When West discarded, declarers took a club finesse to his jack. Down one.

Question: Was there a way to guarantee the contract without 3-3 diamonds?

At the other table, play started the same. But after declarer drew the last trump, he cashed his last trump, discarding a club from dummy. When he tested the diamonds and led the third diamond to dummy, West showed out. Everyone now was reduced to two cards, instead of three.

He led the club from dummy and East played low. What was East's last card? With the diamond jack guarding the diamonds. East can't have the club queen. Declarer played the ace, dropping West's queen.

FINESSE? WHAT'S THE HURRY?

```
                    ♠ A Q 9 7 6 5 3
                    ♡ J 3
                    ◊ Q 3
                    ♣ A 3
    ♠ X 8 4                            ♠ X
    ♡ K Q 8 7                          ♡ 10 9 6 5 4 2
    ◊ 10 8 6 5 4                       ◊ J 9 7 2
    ♣ 7                                ♣ 9 8
                    ♠ J 2
                    ♡ A
                    ◊ A K
                    ♣ K Q J 10 6 5 4 2
```

Contract: 7 ♣

Opening Lead: ♡ King

Declarer won the opening lead, drew trumps and took a spade finesse.

Question: What was the result? How would you have played?

Slower, I hope. What's the big hurry? At the other table, declarer won the heart ace and drew trumps. Then she cashed the A-K of diamonds and started running clubs, being careful to save the heart jack in dummy.

```
With three cards to be played:     ♠ A Q ♡ J ◊ -- ♣ --
♠ X 4 ♡ Q ◊ -- ♣ --                                     ♠ X (x) ♡ (x) 2 ◊ - ♣ -
                        ♠ J 2 ♡ -- ◊ -- ♣ 2
```

Declarer led her last club. West had to discard a spade since dummy had the heart jack. So declarer discarded the heart jack. Now declarer led a spade and West followed.

Did you finesse? What is West's last card? The heart queen. Can he have the spade king? Obviously not, so declarer went up with the spade ace, dropping East's singleton king. She didn't squeeze anyone, it was a "show-up".

FREE

FINESSES

NO FREE FINESSE

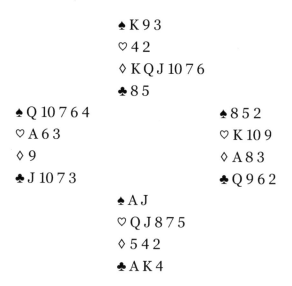

Contract: 3 NT

Opening Lead: ♠ 6

Declarer won the spade jack and counting plenty of tricks, started the diamonds. East held up his ace until the third round. Since declarer had no entry to dummy, those diamonds are still there today.

Question: This was a classic example of what? How would you have played?

At the other table, the declarer counted two spades, two clubs, and five diamonds as long as he could take them. So this was a classic example of "no thanks" and he won the first trick with the ace, turning down the free finesse.

As the other declarer saw, it wasn't so free. This declarer made 3 NT.

AVOIDING FREE FINESSES

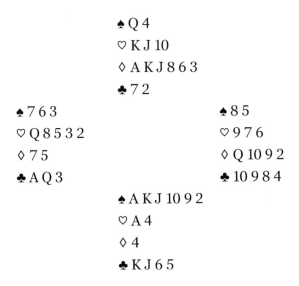

Contract: 6 ♠

Opening Lead: ♡ 3

Dummy's ten won the first trick. Declarer had to draw trumps before trying the diamonds. Then he played the A-K of diamonds, but when the queen did not appear, he had no entry to dummy even if he could set up the diamonds.

Question: How would you have played to make this slam?

The other declarer correctly saw a second suit hand, and therefore entries were important. The 'free' finesse at trick one was not so free. It came with the cost of an entry. Declarer said, "no thanks," and won the first heart trick with the ace.

He cashed the diamond ace and ruffed a diamond. Then the trump ace and a trump to dummy's queen to lead another small diamond, ruffed high.

After drawing the last trump, the heart four in his hand was the way back to dummy's good diamonds.

NO FREE FINESSES

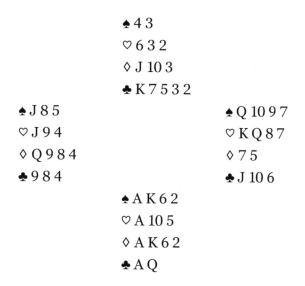

```
                    ♠ 4 3
                    ♡ 6 3 2
                    ◊ J 10 3
                    ♣ K 7 5 3 2
   ♠ J 8 5                          ♠ Q 10 9 7
   ♡ J 9 4                          ♡ K Q 8 7
   ◊ Q 9 8 4                        ◊ 7 5
   ♣ 9 8 4                          ♣ J 10 6
                    ♠ A K 6 2
                    ♡ A 10 5
                    ◊ A K 6 2
                    ♣ A Q
```

Contract: 3 NT
Opening Lead: ◊ 4

Declarer played the jack from dummy which held. He cashed the A-Q of clubs and led a low diamond. West rose with the queen and returned a diamond.

Declarer ended with eight tricks, down one.

Question: Could you have handled your entries in a different fashion?

At the other table, to assure a later entry to those clubs, declarer played low from dummy and won the first diamond trick in his hand with the ace.

Now with the ◊ J-10 still in the dummy and two small diamonds in his hand, West could not prevent declarer from reaching the dummy later.

NO FREE FINESSE, WINNING UNNESSARILY HIGH

```
                        ♠ 9 4
                        ♡ 4 2
                        ◊ Q 6 4
                        ♣ Q J 10 6 5 2
        ♠ 8 5 2                         ♠ Q 10 7 6 3
        ♡ Q 10 8 7                      ♡ A 9 5
        ◊ K 10 8 3 2                    ◊ 9 7
        ♣ 4                             ♣ K 8 7
                        ♠ A K J
                        ♡ K J 6 3
                        ◊ A J 5
                        ♣ A 9 3
```

Contract: 3 NT
Opening Lead: ◊ 3

Declarer won the jack in hand, thinking "thank you" and led the club three. East ducked the first two club tricks, thinking "no, thank you."

Declarer could take a successful major suit finesse, but at best was going to finish with three clubs, two diamonds, and three tricks in the majors.
Down one.

There was no way back to the good clubs. If declarer led a low diamond, West would win blocking the suit.

Question: How would you have untangled this?

Simple. The other declarer received the same opening lead, but she was willing to give up one trick to win five, a pretty good deal. She won the first diamond trick with the ace, not the jack.

Now she had a sure late entry to the dummy to use the clubs. Give one, get five? Pretty good deal.

NO FREE FINESSE

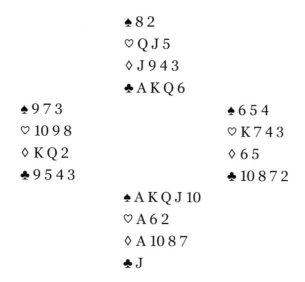

```
              ♠ 8 2
              ♡ Q J 5
              ◊ J 9 4 3
              ♣ A K Q 6
♠ 9 7 3                      ♠ 6 5 4
♡ 10 9 8                     ♡ K 7 4 3
◊ K Q 2                      ◊ 6 5
♣ 9 5 4 3                    ♣ 10 8 7 2
              ♠ A K Q J 10
              ♡ A 6 2
              ◊ A 10 8 7
              ♣ J
```

Contract: 6 ♠

Opening Lead: ♡ 10

Declarer played the queen at trick one, East ducked, and declarer played low, perhaps too quickly? Now he could not untangle the clubs and draw trumps. Only eleven tricks. Down one.

Question: How did the other declarer make the slam with the same lead?

At the other table, declarer gave the hand a little more thought, and saw the need for a later dummy entry. He played low at trick one, giving up on the "free" finesse, since he could afford to lose one heart trick.

Now after drawing trumps and unblocking the club jack, he had a heart entry to the good clubs to discard his diamond losers.

NO FREE FINESSES

```
                    ♠ Q J 10
                    ♡ 7 2
                    ◊ A J 10 9 8 4
                    ♣ 8 3
        ♠ 9 7 6 4                    ♠ K 5 3
        ♡ Q 6 3                      ♡ J 10 8 5
        ◊ 7 3                        ◊ K 5 2
        ♣ Q 7 5 2                    ♣ A 6 4
                    ♠ A 8 2
                    ♡ A K 9 4
                    ◊ Q 6
                    ♣ K J 10 9
```

Contract: 3 NT
Opening Lead: ♠ 4

Declarer played dummy's ten, East played low, the ten winning. Declarer came to his hand with a heart and took a diamond finesse. East ducked one round, and won the second round, exiting a heart.

Declarer had no way to reach dummy. Ace and a small spade would lose, and if declarer led low, East would win, blocking the suit. No 3 NT for this declarer.

Question: Was there a 3 NT for the other declarer?

At the other table, the declarer again made a good exchange. Lose one trick to gain five tricks. He won the first trick with the ace of spades to be assured of a late entry to dummy.

A similar situation would be the following:
Dummy has Q 10 9 and declarer has A J 8. Declarer would need to win the ace to be able to force his way back to dummy later.

212

NO FREE FINESSE

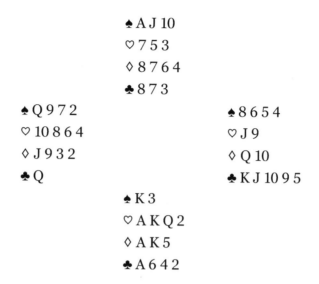

```
              ♠ A J 10
              ♡ 7 5 3
              ◊ 8 7 6 4
              ♣ 8 7 3
♠ Q 9 7 2                    ♠ 8 6 5 4
♡ 10 8 6 4                   ♡ J 9
◊ J 9 3 2                    ◊ Q 10
♣ Q                         ♣ K J 10 9 5
              ♠ K 3
              ♡ A K Q 2
              ◊ A K 5
              ♣ A 6 4 2
```

Contract: 3 NT

Opening Lead: ♠ 2

Dummy's ten won the first trick. Then trying to find a ninth trick, he played the A-K of diamonds, but they were 4-2. He finished with eight tricks.

Down one.

North asked South, "How did you compress your nine tricks into eight?"

Question: What did North mean? How would you have found a ninth trick?

The other declarer counted his tricks, but counted three spade tricks, as long as he won the first spade trick in hand.

After testing the diamonds, he could take a spade finesse against West which was a big favorite to win.

A FREE FINESSE? NO THANKS

```
                    ♠ K J 7 6 3
                    ♡ Q 7 3
                    ◊ 4 3
                    ♣ J 4 2
    ♠ 4                             ♠ 10 9 8 5 2
    ♡ A 10 8 6 4                    ♡ 5 2
    ◊ Q 9 2                         ◊ J 10 8 5
    ♣ Q 10 6 5                      ♣ K 7
                    ♠ A Q
                    ♡ K J 9
                    ◊ A K 7 6
                    ♣ A 9 8 3
```

Contract: 3 NT

Opening Lead: ♡ 6

Declarer won the opening lead with the nine, perhaps too quickly. He played the A-Q of spades, but West showed out, so overtaking was not an option. He needed four spade tricks, not three. He needed to get to dummy, but the only entry was the heart queen.

If he led the heart jack, West would win the ace and the suit was blocked. If he led the king, West would duck. He tried the jack, West won.

No 3 NT for this declarer.

Question: How would you have made your way back to dummy?

The other declarer used the Rule of Eleven. West was marked with all the hearts higher than the six. The heart queen was a sure entry as long as declarer kept two cards lower than the queen.

He won trick one with the king of hearts. West could not prevent him from later reaching dummy and the good spades.

SECOND SUIT ENTRIES: NO FINESSES, THANKS ANYHOW

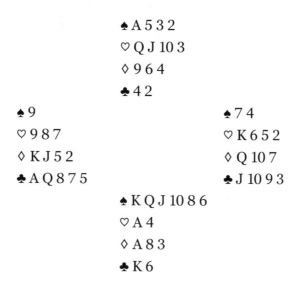

♠ A 5 3 2
♡ Q J 10 3
♦ 9 6 4
♣ 4 2

♠ 9
♡ 9 8 7
♦ K J 5 2
♣ A Q 8 7 5

♠ 7 4
♡ K 6 5 2
♦ Q 10 7
♣ J 10 9 3

♠ K Q J 10 8 6
♡ A 4
♦ A 8 3
♣ K 6

Contract: 4 ♠

Opening Lead: ♡ 9

Declarer played the queen at trick one, but East saw no reason to cover. "Thank you," said the declarer to himself. He drew trumps and led a club to his king. West cashed two club tricks, and played another heart.

The two good hearts are still sitting in the dummy. Declarer lost two diamonds at the end. Down one.

Question: How would you have untangled the entries?

At the other table, declarer received the same opening lead. Declarer said to himself "No thanks," and played low from dummy, winning the ace. He cashed the K-Q of trumps and led his low heart.

The defense took one heart and two clubs, but the trump ace was the entry to the two good hearts. Declarer discarded his diamond losers, making four spades.

No free finesses, thanks.

UNUSUAL

FINESSES

BACKWARDS FINESSE

$$\spadesuit\ K\ Q\ J\ 7\ 3$$
$$\heartsuit\ Q\ 3$$
$$\diamond\ Q\ 4\ 3$$
$$\clubsuit\ A\ 5\ 3$$

♠ 9 5		♠ 8 6 2
♡ K 10 6 4		♡ 8 7 5
◊ J 10 9 6		◊ 8 5 2
♣ 9 4 2		♣ K 8 7 6

$$\spadesuit\ A\ 10\ 4$$
$$\heartsuit\ A\ J\ 9\ 2$$
$$\diamond\ A\ K\ 7$$
$$\clubsuit\ Q\ J\ 10$$

Contract: 6 NT
Opening Lead: ◊ Jack

Declarer won the opening lead in dummy and led the heart queen, losing to West's king. He won the diamond return and cashed the A-J of hearts. When the heart ten did not fall, he took a club finesse. Down one.

"Both finesses lost, partner," moaned South. "I am just unlucky."
"How do you think I feel," thought North to himself.
"Can't you at least try the correct finesse?" asked North.

Question: What finesse was North referring to?

The other declarer won the opening lead in hand. He took a heart finesse but in the other direction, by leading towards the queen. If West had the king and took it, declarer had twelve tricks.

If West ducked, declarer had five spades, two hearts, three diamonds, and two or three clubs.

If East won the heart king, declarer could still try to drop the heart ten, or then try the club finesse as a LAST RESORT.

217

BACKWARDS FINESSE

♠ A Q 6 2
♡ J 2
♢ A 5 2
♣ J 6 5 3

♠ 8   ♠ 9 4
♡ Q 9 3   ♡ 10 8 7 6
♢ K J 10 9 4   ♢ 7 6
♣ A K 9 8   ♣ Q 10 7 4 2

♠ K J 10 7 5 3
♡ A K 5 4
♢ Q 8 3
♣ ----

South	West	North	East	
1 ♠	Dbl	2 NT*	P	* Limit raise or better
4 ♣^	P	4 ♢	P	^ Shortness
6 ♠		All Pass		

Opening Lead: ♣ King

Declarer ruffed the opening lead and drew trumps. With two possible diamond losers, he led a diamond to his queen. He finished down one, losing two diamonds.

"Please don't tell me about your bad luck again," said North. "Go buy Dr J's book and maybe you will start taking the correct finesses."

Question: What finesse was North referring to?

The other declarer saw the futility of leading to the diamond queen. West was a big favorite to hold the diamond king. But West was also a big favorite to hold another significant card.

After drawing trumps, he led a low heart towards dummy's jack. He lost a trick in a suit he started with no losers, but he gained two tricks.

West won the heart queen, but declarer discarded dummy's diamond losers on the hearts. Making six spades, losing an unexpected heart but no diamonds.

BACKWARDS FINESSE

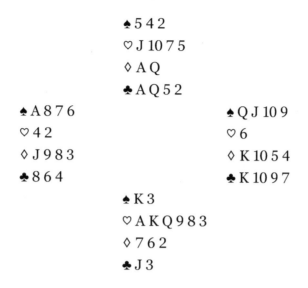

♠ 5 4 2
♡ J 10 7 5
◊ A Q
♣ A Q 5 2

♠ A 8 7 6
♡ 4 2
◊ J 9 8 3
♣ 8 6 4

♠ Q J 10 9
♡ 6
◊ K 10 5 4
♣ K 10 9 7

♠ K 3
♡ A K Q 9 8 3
◊ 7 6 2
♣ J 3

Contract: 4 ♡

Opening Lead: ♡ 2

Declarer won the opening lead and drew trumps. He led the jack of clubs for a finesse. East won and shifted to spades. The defense took two spade tricks. When declarer later took a diamond finesse, he was down one.

"Three losing finesses," moaned South. "You took all the finesses you didn't need, and not the one you should have," responded North.

Question: Which finesse did South miss? He took a lot of them.

The above declarer was going in the wrong direction. He needed to go backwards, not forwards. After drawing trumps, the other declarer led a low club towards the jack, going the opposite way.

If East had the king, declarer could discard two diamonds on the A-Q of clubs, losing only one club and two spades.

If West had the king, declarer was safe. If West returned a diamond, declarer could play the ace, and discard one spade on a high club. He would lose one spade, one diamond, and one club.

DEEP FINESSE

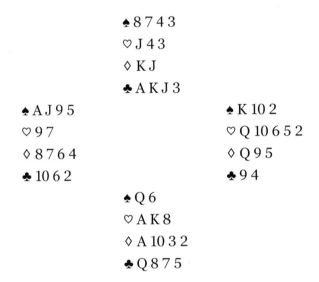

```
                  ♠ 8 7 4 3
                  ♡ J 4 3
                  ◊ K J
                  ♣ A K J 3
      ♠ A J 9 5                   ♠ K 10 2
      ♡ 9 7                       ♡ Q 10 6 5 2
      ◊ 8 7 6 4                   ◊ Q 9 5
      ♣ 10 6 2                    ♣ 9 4
                  ♠ Q 6
                  ♡ A K 8
                  ◊ A 10 3 2
                  ♣ Q 8 7 5
```

Contract: 3 NT
Opening Lead: ♡ 9

Declarer counted eight top tricks. He tried for a ninth trick by taking a diamond finesse, low to the jack. East won and shifted to spades. Down one.

Question: Unlucky? It was a 50/50 guess.

The other declarer, after the same opening lead, saw a much better chance than the diamond finesse. At trick one, he played the heart jack. East covered with the queen and declarer won.

He went to dummy with a club and led a heart. When East played low, declarer played the eight.

Game over, nine tricks.

DEEP FINESSE

```
              ♠ J 9 3
              ♡ 5 3
              ◊ 10 4 2
              ♣ K Q J 6 4
   ♠ 10 7 5                    ♠ K 8 2
   ♡ 9 7 2                     ♡ J 10 8 6 4
   ◊ 9 3                       ◊ A K Q
   ♣ 10 9 7 5 2                ♣ 8 3
              ♠ A Q 6 4
              ♡ A K Q
              ◊ J 8 7 6 5
              ♣ A
```

East	South	West	North
1 ♡	Dbl	P	2 ♣
P	2 NT	P	3 NT
	All Pass		

Opening Lead: ♡ 2

Declarer won the opening lead and counted his tricks. He could try the diamonds or the clubs. But getting to the clubs seemed impossible, for surely the spade jack was not an entry. East had to have the king for his opening bid.

After taking forever, he finished down one.

Question: Eight tricks. Any chance for a ninth trick?

At the other table, the declarer saw the hand the same way. But he cashed the club ace and led a spade to the nine.

He had three spades, three hearts, and four clubs. Making 3 NT

DEEP FINESSE

```
                        ♠ A
                        ♡ 10 9 3
                        ◇ 9 8 6 5 3
                        ♣ 8 6 5 3
        ♠ Q 10 7 4 3                       ♠ 9 8 6 5 2
        ♡ 8 5 4                            ♡ A J 7 6
        ◇ K 10 7                           ◇ A 4
        ♣ 10 4                             ♣ 7 2
                        ♠ K J
                        ♡ K Q 2
                        ◇ Q J 2
                        ♣ A K Q J 9
```

Contract: 3 NT
Opening Lead: ♠ 4

Declarer won in dummy and played a heart to his king, which won. He led the diamond queen, but the defenders won and continued spades.

Declarer had only eight tricks. Down one.

Question: Where is there a ninth trick?

The other declarer saw a 50% chance. At trick two, he led the heart ten and when East played low, he played low. If it won or knocked out the heart ace, he had nine tricks.

If not, on to the next hand. Nothing ventured, nothing gained.

DEEP FINESSE

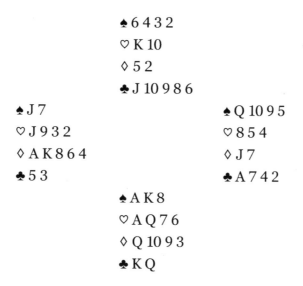

```
                    ♠ 6 4 3 2
                    ♡ K 10
                    ◊ 5 2
                    ♣ J 10 9 8 6
    ♠ J 7                           ♠ Q 10 9 5
    ♡ J 9 3 2                       ♡ 8 5 4
    ◊ A K 8 6 4                     ◊ J 7
    ♣ 5 3                           ♣ A 7 4 2
                    ♠ A K 8
                    ♡ A Q 7 6
                    ◊ Q 10 9 3
                    ♣ K Q
```

Contract: 3 NT
Opening Lead: ◊ 6

Declarer won the opening lead with his queen. He led the K-Q of clubs, the opponents ducked twice. Declarer had only eight tricks. He played the A-K of spades and another spade, a 35% chance of a 3-3 split.

When spades were 4-2, declarer finished with eight tricks. Down one.

Question: After the good defense, could you have succeeded?

The first three tricks were the same at the other table. But to increase the odds of success from 35% to 50%, declarer led a heart to the ten.

Success, maybe with more than nine tricks. That's life at the table. Somedays chicken, somedays feathers.

GOING DEEP

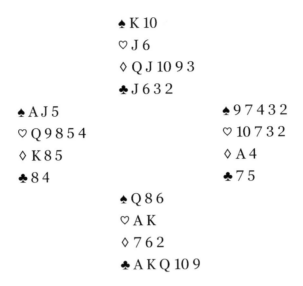

♠ K 10
♥ J 6
♦ Q J 10 9 3
♣ J 6 3 2

♠ A J 5
♥ Q 9 8 5 4
♦ K 8 5
♣ 8 4

♠ 9 7 4 3 2
♥ 10 7 3 2
♦ A 4
♣ 7 5

♠ Q 8 6
♥ A K
♦ 7 6 2
♣ A K Q 10 9

Contract: 3 NT
Opening Lead: ♥ 5

Declarer won the opening lead and counted eight tricks, including one spade. He started the diamonds, the obvious source of tricks. But he was in a race he could not win, being one step behind.

The opponents set up the hearts before he could set up and use the diamonds. Down one.

Question: Could you have made it to the finish line ahead of the defenders?

At the other table, the declarer was not going to enter a race he could not win. Risking going down an extra trick, he won the opening lead and played a spade to the ten.

He won the race with two spades, two hearts, and five clubs.

DEEP FINESSE

                        ♠ J 10 3
                        ♡ K 10 4 2
                        ◊ K Q 10 5
                        ♣ 10 5

        ♠ 7 5 4 2   ♠ A K
        ♡ 8   ♡ Q 9 6 5 3
        ◊ 8 6 2   ◊ 9 3
        ♣ Q J 8 4 3   ♣ A 9 7 2

                        ♠ Q 9 8 6
                        ♡ A J 7
                        ◊ A J 7 4
                        ♣ K 6

East	South	West	North
1 ♡	1 NT	P	3 NT
	All Pass		

Opening Lead: ♣ 4

East won the opening lead and returned a club. With the clubs ready to run, there was no chance of getting any spade tricks. Needing eight red suit tricks, declarer played a heart to the jack. It won, but declarer had only eight tricks. Down one.

Question: Is there a road to nine tricks after a club lead?

With East marked with at least five hearts, perhaps West has a singleton eight or nine of hearts. Declarer led the ten of hearts from dummy.

If East did not cover, he would next finesse the jack for four heart tricks. So East had to cover. When West's eight fell under the ten, queen, ace, declarer went back to dummy using diamonds as transportation.

He now had ♡ K 4 2 in dummy and ♡ J 7 in hand over East's ♡ 9 6 5 3. He won four hearts, four diamonds, and one club. Making 3 NT.

FINESSE DOOMED? TRY AN INTRA – FINESSE

```
                        ♠ ----
                        ♡ A 8 4 2
                        ◇ 6 4 2
                        ♣ A J 7 6 4 2
            ♠ A Q 10 4 3                  ♠ K 8 7 6 2
            ♡ Q 6 5                       ♡ 10 7 3
            ◇ K 9 7 5                     ◇ Q 3
            ♣ 8                           ♣ Q 10 5
                        ♠ J 9 5
                        ♡ K J 9
                        ◇ A J 10 8
                        ♣ K 9 3
```

South	West	North	East
1 ◇	1 ♠	2 ♣	2 ♠
3 ♣	P	5 ♣	All Pass

Opening Lead: ♠ Ace

Declarer ruffed the opening lead. He cashed the A – K of trumps and took a diamond finesse, losing to West's king. A second diamond finesse was successful, but when he later played a heart to the jack, West won the queen.

Down one, losing one heart, one diamond, and one club.

Question: Just unlucky or could you have done better?

The other declarer reasoned after East showed up with a probable spade honor and both minor queens, that almost surely West had the heart queen.

He took an intra-finesse, by leading the heart jack. When West covered, he won the ace and led towards his ♡ K 9, and finessed East for the ten.
Making five clubs.

YOU KNOW YOUR FINESSE WILL LOSE?
TRY AN INTRA - FINESSE

```
                        ♠ K Q 8 2
                        ♡ A 8 6
                        ◊ K J 9
                        ♣ 10 9 4
        ♠ 6 5                               ♠ 7 3
        ♡ Q J 10 2                          ♡ K 7 5 4
        ◊ 10 6 3                            ◊ Q 8 7
        ♣ A K 6 3                           ♣ J 8 7 2
                        ♠ A J 10 9 4
                        ♡ 9 3
                        ◊ A 5 4 2
                        ♣ Q 5
```

West	North	East	South
P	1 ♣	P	1 ♠
P	2 ♠	P	4 ♠
	All Pass		

Opening Lead: ♣ Ace

West cashed the A-K of clubs and switched to the heart queen. Declarer won the ace and drew trumps. He led a diamond to the jack. East won and the defense cashed a heart. Down one.

Question: Any other line of play? Was the contract always doomed?

At the other table, play started the same. After declarer drew trumps, she reasoned that since she had already seen ten HCP's in the West hand, the A-K of clubs, the queen and presumed jack of hearts, that the diamond finesse was offsides.

But what about the diamond ten? She took an intra-finesse. She led the diamond jack. East covered (if not, declarer would have played low), declarer won the ace, and led a low diamond towards dummy's ◆ K 9. She finessed West for the diamond ten and made four spades.

AN INTRA – FINESSE BY INFERENCE

```
                        ♠ A 4 2
                        ♡ J 8
                        ◇ Q 8 7 5 4
                        ♣ Q 9 3
           ♠ Q 7 3                        ♠ 10 6
           ♡ A 7 2                        ♡ K 5 4 3
           ◇ A J 2                        ◇ K 10 3
           ♣ 10 8 5 4                     ♣ K J 7 6
                        ♠ K J 9 8 5
                        ♡ Q 10 9 6
                        ◇ 9 6
                        ♣ A 2
```

North	East	South	West
P	P	1 ♠	P
2 ♠		All Pass	

Opening Lead: ♣ 4

At trick one, West led a club, queen, king, ace. Declarer led a spade to the ace and a spade to his jack. West won the queen. The defense cashed the A-K of hearts and A-K of diamonds, and the club jack. Down one.

Question: How did the other declarer play to make two spades?

At trick two, the other declarer wasn't ready to play trumps, but needed more information. He played a heart, East won the king and cashed the club jack. Declarer ruffed the next club.

Now declarer knew the following. He presumed the A-K of diamonds were divided from the opening lead. East had shown the king of hearts and the K-J of clubs. With a high diamond and the spade queen, East would have opened the bidding. So a trump to the jack was unlikely to succeed.

Declarer tried an intra-finesse. He led the spade jack. West had to cover. Declarer won, and finessed East for the spade ten.

Making two spades, losing two hearts, two diamonds, and one club.

Printed in the United States
by Baker & Taylor Publisher Services